THE WORSHIPFUL MASTER'S

SPECIAL HELP;

A MONITOR FOR

THE MASTER OF THE LODGE;

CONTAINING

All information proper to be published, which is necessary to qualify him for the important duties of his station.

———— ◦ ● ◦ ————

"If a man vow a vow unto the Lord, or swear an oath to bind his soul with a bond, *he shall not break his word; he shall do according to all that proceedeth out of his mouth.*"—NUMBERS XXX. 2,

———— ●◦● ————

British Library Cataloguing-in-Publication Data
A catalogue record for this book is available from
the British Library

PRELIMINARY.

THE ORIGIN AND PROGRESS OF FREEMASONRY.

ANY inquiry into the symbolism and philosophy of Freemasonry must necessarily be preceded by a brief investigation of the origin and history of the institution. Ancient and universal as it is, whence did it arise? What were the accidents connected with its birth? From what kindred or similar association did it spring? Or was it original and autochthonic, independent, in its inception, of any external influences, and unconnected with any other institution? These are questions which an intelligent investigator will be disposed to propound in the very commencement of the inquiry, and they are questions which must be distinctly answered before he can be expected to comprehend its true character as a symbolic institution. He must know something of its antecedents before he can appreciate its character.

But he who expects to arrive at a satisfactory solution of this inquiry must first — as a preliminary absolutely necessary to success — release himself from the influence of an error into which novices in Masonic philosophy are too apt to fall. He must not confound the doctrine of Freemasonry with its outward and extrinsic form. He must not suppose that certain usages and ceremonies, which exist at this day, but which, even now, are subject to extensive variations in different countries, constitute the sum and substance of Freemasonry. " Prudent antiquity," says Lord Coke, " did for more solemnity and better memory and observation of that which is to be done, express substances under ceremonies." But it must be always remembered that the ceremony is not the substance. It is but the outer garment which covers and perhaps adorns it, as clothing does the human figure. But divest man of that outward apparel, and you still have the microcosm, the wondrous creation, with all his nerves, and bones, and muscles, and, above all, with his brain, and thoughts, and feelings. And so take from Masonry these external ceremonies, and you still have remaining its philosophy and science. These have, of course, always continued the same, while the ceremonies have varied in different ages, and still vary in different countries.

The definition of Freemasonry that it is " a science of morality, veiled in allegory, and illustrated by symbols," has been so often quoted, that, were it not for its beauty, it would become wearisome. But this definition contains the exact principle that has just been enunciated. Freemasonry is a science — a philosophy — a system of doctrines which is taught, in a manner peculiar to itself, by allegories and symbols. This is its internal character. Its ceremonies are external additions, which affect not its substance.

Now, when we are about to institute an inquiry into the origin of Freemasonry, it is of this peculiar system of philosophy that we are to inquire, and not of the ceremonies which have been foisted on it. If we pursue any other course we shall assuredly fall into error.

Thus, if we seek the origin and first beginning of the Masonic philosophy, we must go away back into the ages of remote antiquity, when we shall find this beginning in the bosom of kindred associations, where the same philosophy was maintained and taught. But if we confound the ceremonies of Masonry with the philosophy of Masonry, and seek the origin of the institution, moulded into outward form as it is to-day, we can scarcely be required to look farther back than the beginning of the eighteenth century, and, indeed, not quite so far. For many important modifications have been made in its rituals since that period.

Having, then, arrived at the conclusion that it is not the Masonic ritual, but the Masonic philosophy, whose origin we are to investigate, the next question naturally relates to the peculiar nature of that philosophy.

Now, then, I contend that the philosophy of Freemasonry is engaged in the contemplation of the divine and human character; of GOD as one eternal, self-existent being, in contradiction to the mythology of the ancient peoples, which was burdened with a multitude of gods and goddesses, of demigods and heroes; of MAN as an immortal being, preparing in the present life for an eternal future, in like contradiction to the ancient philosophy, which circumscribed the existence of man to the pres ent life.

These two doctrines, then, of the unity of God and the

immortality of the soul, constitute the philosophy of Free-masonry. When we wish to define it succinctly, we say that it is an ancient system of philosophy which teaches these two dogmas. And hence, if, amid the intellectual darkness and debasement of the old polytheistic religions, we find interspersed here and there, in all ages, certain institutions or associations which taught these truths, and that, in a particular way, allegorically and symbolically, then we have a right to say that such institutions or associations were the incunabula — the predecessors — of the Masonic institution as it now exists.

With these preliminary remarks the reader will be enabled to enter upon the consideration of that theory of the origin of Freemasonry which I advance in the following propositions : —

1. In the first place, I contend that in the very earliest ages of the world there were existent certain truths of vast importance to the welfare and happiness of humanity, which had been communicated, — no matter how, but, — most probably, by direct inspiration from God to man.

2. These truths principally consisted in the abstract propositions of the unity of God and the immortality of the soul. Of the truth of these two propositions there cannot be a reasonable doubt. The belief in these truths is a necessary consequence of that religious sentiment which has always formed an essential feature of human nature. Man is, emphatically, and in distinction from all other creatures, a religious animal. Gross commences his interesting work on " The Heathen Religion in its Popular and Symbolical Development " by the statement that " one of the most remarkable phenomena of the

human race is the universal existence of religious ideas —
a belief in something supernatural and divine, and a
worship corresponding to it." As nature had implanted
the religious sentiment, the same nature must have directed it in a proper channel. The belief and the worship must at first have been as pure as the fountain whence
they flowed, although, in subsequent times, and before the
advent of Christian light, they may both have been cor-
rupted by the influence of the priests and the poets over
an ignorant and superstitious people. The first and second propositions of my theory refer only to that primeval
period which was antecedent to these corruptions, of
which I shall hereafter speak.

3. These truths of God and immortality were most
probably handed down through the line of patriarchs
of the race of Seth, but were, at all events, known to
Noah, and were by him communicated to his immediate
descendants.

4. In consequence of this communication, the true
worship of God continued, for some time after the sub-
sidence of the deluge, to be cultivated by the Noachidæ,
the Noachites, or the descendants of Noah.

5. At a subsequent period (no matter when, but the
biblical record places it at the attempted building of the
tower of Babel), there was a secession of a large number
of the human race from the Noachites.

6. These seceders rapidly lost sight of the divine truths
which had been communicated to them from their common ancestor, and fell into the most grievous theological
errors, corrupting the purity of the worship and the
orthodoxy of the religious faith which they had primarily received.

7. These truths were preserved in their integrity by but a very few in the patriarchal line, while still fewer were enabled to retain only dim and glimmering portions of the true light.

8. The first class was confined to the direct descendants of Noah, and the second was to be found among the priests and philosophers, and, perhaps, still later. among the poets of the heathen nations, and among those whom they initiated into the secrets of these truths. Of the prevalence of these religious truths among the patriarchal descendants of Noah, we have ample evidence in the sacred records. As to their existence among a body of learned heathens, we have the testimony of many intelligent writers who have devoted their energies to this subject. Thus the learned Grote, in his "History of Greece," says, "The allegorical interpretation of the myths has been, by several learned investigators, especially by Creuzer, connected with the hypothesis of *an ancient and highly instructed body of priests*, having their origin either in Egypt or in the East, and communicating to the rude and barbarous Greeks religious, physical, and historical knowledge, *under the veil of symbols.*" What is here said only of the Greeks is equally applicable to every other intellectual nation of antiquity.

9. The system or doctrine of the former class has been called by Masonic writers the "Pure or Primitive Freemasonry" of antiquity, and that of the latter class the "Spurious Freemasonry" of the same period. These terms were first used, if I mistake not, by Dr. Oliver, and are intended to refer — the word *pure* to the doctrines taught by the descendants of Noah in the Jewish

line, and the word *spurious* to his descendants in the heathen or Gentile line.

10. The masses of the people, among the Gentiles especially, were totally unacquainted with this divine truth, which was the foundation stone of both species of Freemasonry, the pure and the spurious, and were deeply immersed in the errors and falsities of heathen belief and worship.

11. These errors of the heathen religions were not the voluntary inventions of the peoples who cultivated them, but were gradual and almost unavoidable corruptions of the truths which had been at first taught by Noah ; and, indeed, so palpable are these corruptions, that they can be readily detected and traced to the original form from which, however much they might vary among different peoples, they had, at one time or another, deviated. Thus, in the life and achievements of Bacchus or Dionysus, we find the travestied counterpart of the career of Moses, and in the name of Vulcan, the blacksmith god, we evidently see an etymological corruption of the appellation of Tubal Cain, the first artificer in metals. For *Vul-can* is but a modified form of *Baal-Cain*, the god Cain.

12. But those among the masses — and there were some — who were made acquainted with the truth, received their knowledge by means of an initiation into certain sacred Mysteries, in the bosom of which it was concealed from the public gaze.

13. These Mysteries existed in every country of heathendom, in each under a different name, and to some extent under a different form, but always and everywhere with the same design of inculcating, by allegorical and

symbolic teachings, the great Masonic doctrines of the unity of God and the immortality of the soul. This is an important proposition, and the fact which it enunciates must never be lost sight of in any inquiry into the origin of Freemasonry; for the pagan Mysteries were to the spurious Freemasonry of antiquity precisely what the Masters' lodges are to the Freemasonry of the present day. It is needless to offer any proof of their existence, since this is admitted and continually referred to by all historians, ancient and modern; and to discuss minutely their character and organization would occupy a distinct treatise. The Baron de Sainte Croix has written two large volumes on the subject, and yet left it unexhausted.

14. These two divisions of the Masonic Institution which were defined in the 9th proposition, namely, the pure or primitive Freemasonry among the Jewish descendants of the patriarchs, who are called, by way of distinction, the Noachites, or descendants of Noah, because they had not forgotten nor abandoned the teachings of their great ancestor, and the spurious Freemasonry practised among the pagan nations, flowed down the stream of time in parallel currents, often near together, but never commingling.

15. But these two currents were not always to be kept apart, for, springing, in the long anterior ages, from one common fountain, — that ancient priesthood of whom I have already spoken in the 8th proposition, — and then dividing into the pure and spurious Freemasonry of antiquity, and remaining separated for centuries upon centuries, they at length met at the building of the great temple of Jerusalem, and were united, in the instance of the Israelites under King Solomon, and the Tyrians

under Hiram, King of Tyre, and Hiram Abif. The spurious Freemasonry, it is true, did not then and there cease to exist. On the contrary, it lasted for centuries subsequent to this period; for it was not until long after, and in the reign of the Emperor Theodosius, that the pagan Mysteries were finally and totally abolished. But by the union of the Jewish or pure Freemasons and the Tyrian or spurious Freemasons at Jerusalem, there was a mutual infusion of their respective doctrines and ceremonies, which eventually terminated in the abolition of the two distinctive systems and the establishment of a new one, that may be considered as the immediate prototype of the present institution. Hence many Masonic students, going no farther back in their investigations than the facts announced in this 15th proposition, are content to find the origin of Freemasonry at the temple of Solomon. But if my theory be correct, the truth is, that it there received, not its birth, but only a new modification of its character. The legend of the third degree — the golden legend, the *legenda aurea* — of Masonry was there adopted by pure Freemasonry, which before had no such legend, from spurious Freemasonry. But the legend had existed under other names and forms, in all the Mysteries, for ages before. The doctrine of immortality, which had hitherto been taught by the Noachites simply as an abstract proposition, was thenceforth to be inculcated by a symbolic lesson — the symbol of Hiram the Builder was to become forever after the distinctive feature of Freemasonry.

16. But another important modification was effected in the Masonic system at the building of the temple. Previous to the union which then took place, the pure Free-

masonry of the Noachites had always been speculative, but resembled the present organization in no other way than in the cultivation of the same abstract principles of divine truth.

17. The Tyrians, on the contrary, were architects by profession, and, as their leaders were disciples of the school of the spurious Freemasonry, they, for the first time, at the temple of Solomon, when they united with their Jewish contemporaries, infused into the speculative science, which was practised by the latter, the elements of an operative art.

18. Therefore the system continued thenceforward, for ages, to present the commingled elements of operative and speculative Masonry. We see this in the *Collegia Fabrorum*, or Colleges of Artificers, first established at Rome by Numa, and which were certainly of a Masonic form in their organization; in the Jewish sect of the Essenes, who wrought as well as prayed, and who are claimed to have been the descendants of the temple builders, and also, and still more prominently, in the Travelling Freemasons of the middle ages, who identify themselves by their very name with their modern successors, and whose societies were composed of learned men who thought and wrote, and of workmen who labored and built. And so for a long time Freemasonry continued to be both operative and speculative.

19. But another change was to be effected in the institution to make it precisely what it now is, and, therefore, at a very recent period (comparatively speaking), the operative feature was abandoned, and Freemasonry became wholly speculative. The exact time of this change is not left to conjecture. It took place in the reign of

Queen Anne, of England, in the beginning of the eighteenth century. Preston gives us the very words of the
decree which established this change, for he says that at
that time it was agreed to " that the privileges of Masonry
should no longer be restricted to operative Masons, but
extend to men of various professions, provided they were
regularly approved and initiated into the order."

The nineteen propositions here announced contain a
brief but succinct view of the progress of Freemasonry
from its origin in the early ages of the world, simply as a
system of religious philosophy, through all the modifications to which it was submitted in the Jewish and Gentile
races, until at length it was developed in its present perfected form. During all this time it preserved unchange-
ably certain features that may hence be considered as its
specific characteristics, by which it has always been distinguished from every other contemporaneous association,
however such association may have simulated it in outward form. These characteristics are, first, the doctrines
which it has constantly taught, namely, that of the unity
of God and that of the immortality of the soul ; and, sec-
ondly, the manner in which these doctrines have been
taught, namely, by symbols and allegories.

Taking these characteristics as the exponents of what
Freemasonry is, we cannot help arriving at the conclusion that the speculative Masonry of the present day ex-
hibits abundant evidence of the identity of its origin with
the spurious Freemasonry of the ante-Solomonic period,
both systems coming from the same pure source, but the
one always preserving, and the other continually corrupting, the purity of the common fountain.

There is also abundant evidence in the history, of which these propositions are but a meagre outline, that a manifest influence was exerted on the pure or primitive Freemasonry of the Noachites by the Tyrian branch of the spurious system, in the symbols, myths, and legends which the former received from the latter, but which it so modified and interpreted as to make them consistent with its own religious system. One thing, at least, is incapable of refutation; and that is, that we are indebted to the Tyrian Masons for the introduction of the symbol of Hiram Abif. The idea of the symbol, although modified by the Jewish Masons, is not Jewish in its inception. It was evidently borrowed from the pagan mysteries, where Bacchus, Adonis, Proserpine, and a host of other apotheosized beings play the same rôle that Hiram does in the Masonic mysteries.

And lastly, we find in the technical terms of Masonry, in its working tools, in the names of its grades, and in a large majority of its symbols, ample testimony of the strong infusion into its religious philosophy of the elements of an operative art. And history again explains this fact by referring to the connection of the institution with the Dionysiac Fraternity of Artificers, who were engaged in building the temple of Solomon, with the Workmen's Colleges of Numa, and with the Travelling Freemasons of the middle ages, who constructed all the great buildings of that period.

These nineteen propositions, which have been submitted in the present essay, constitute a brief summary or outline of a theory of the true origin of Freemasonry, which long and patient investigation has led me to adopt. To attempt to prove the truth of each of these propositions in its order by logical demonstration, or by historical evidence, would involve the writing of an elaborate treatise. They are now offered simply as suggestions on which the Masonic student may ponder. They are but intended as guide-posts, which may direct him in his journey should he undertake the pleasant although difficult task of instituting an inquiry into the origin and progress of Freemasonry from its birth to its present state of full-grown manhood.

But even in this abridged form they are absolutely necessary as preliminary to any true understanding of the symbolism of Freemasonry.

An excerpt from Symbolism of Freemasonry - Explaining it's Science and Philosophy, It's Legends, Myths and Symbols.
- Albert G. Mackey, M. D.

CONTENTS.

———•••———

PREFACE.

———●———

"Whatsoever doth make manifest, is light," says the Sacred Record. We make the application; he to whom all look for instruction should be well instructed; to whom all look for light should himself be enlightened.

"To make manifest" is emphatically the Master's business; to make manifest the emblems, the covenants, the dramatic ceremonies, the entire ends and aims of the Masonic institution. A grand and exalted privilege; a weighty and responsible charge.

One who has been successively Master of several Lodges and tripped at the stumbling blocks which lie in that dark and difficult path, offers in the present volume, the results of his own experience and, through large communications with his fellows, the experience of many others. There is nothing *advised* in this volume that has not been *tried;* nothing been *tried* that has not *succeeded.*

The worst of all the errors into which the many dull and discouraged Lodge Masters run, is that of continuing in the rut made by their predecessors. Nothing good can be expected from a Master who feels bound to follow every usage, right or wrong, established by those who have occupied the

East before him.. If a man who has been elected by the free suffrage of his brethren—who can claim, through his affiliation as Past Master, the countenance and support of every ruler in his jurisdiction, from the Grand Master down— who is denominated by a title " Master" that expresses more than " Prophet, Priest or King," if such a man, himself under the weightiest obligations to do his duty to the Craft without fear or favor, dare not assume the powers symbolized by his gavel, his station, and his title, all counsel and warning are but wasted upon him.

But from those Masters, be they young or old, learned or unlearned, who feel the weight of their official responsibilities, and determine, by every light available to them, that they will neither merit the title of *sluggard* nor *inno- vater*, much may be expected that will equally honor themselves, their Lodges and the Craft universal. For such men his volume has been prepared.

THE WORSHIPFUL MASTER'S

SPECIAL HELP.

CHAPTER I.

THE DESIGNS UPON THE TRESTLE BOARD.

You have been elected by the free suffrages of your fellow members to govern them as their Master for the constitutional term of twelve months, or " until your successor has been duly elected and installed." * You have solemnly accepted this trust. By the most impressive ceremonies known to Ancient Craft Masonry, you were installed into the Chair of King Solomon, and voluntarily assumed pledges of which the following is a synopsis:

---

* In Tennessee, and perhaps one or two other Grand Lodge jurisdictions, the practice of semi-annual elections, formerly quite general, still obtains. Kentucky abandoned it in 1857— other Grand Lodges still earlier. It is destructive to that genuine incentive to mental exertion so essential in forming the MODEL MASTER.

" 1. That you will be a good man and true, and strictly obey the Moral Law.*

2. That you will be a peaceable subject, and cheerfully con‍form to the laws of the country in which you reside.

3. That you will not be concerned in plots and conspiracies against government, but patiently submit to the decisions of the supreme legislature.

4. That you will pay a proper respect to the civil magistrate, will work diligently, live creditably, and act honestly by all men.

5. That you will hold in veneration the original Rulers and Patrons of the Order of Masonry,† and their regular successors, supreme and subordinate, according to their stations, and will submit to the awards and resolutions of your brethren when convened‡ in every case consistent with the constitutions of the Order.§

6. That you will avoid private piques and quarrels, and guard against intemperance and excess.

---

* The " Moral Law" is the Holy Scriptures, presented to the Master at his instalation, especially those of the Old Testa‍ment, the gist of which is found in the Ten Commandments, which, in a peculiar sense, constitute *the Moral Law.*

† These imply King Solomon and the two Hirams, who repre‍sented the pillars of Wisdom, Strength and Beauty in the formation of the Masonic system.

‡ That is, "When in Lodge or Grand Lodge assembled."

§ No legislation upon topics outside of the ancient consti‍tutions is binding upon the Craft.

7. That you will be cautious in carriage and behavior, courteous to your brethren, and faithful to your Lodge.

8. That you will respect genuine brethren, discountenance imposters, and all dissenters from the original plan of Masonry.

9. That you will promote the general good of society, cultivate the social virtues, and propagate the knowledge of the art.

10. That you will pay homage to the Grand Master for the time being, and to his officers when duly installed, and will strictly conform to every edict of the Grand Lodge, or General Assembly of Masons, that is not subversive of the principles and ground-work of Masonry.

11. That you consent to the landmark that it is not in the power of any man or body of men to make innovations in the body of Masonry.

12. That you promise a regular attendance on the committees, and communications of the Grand Lodge, on receiving proper notice,* and will pay attention to all the duties of Masonry on convenient occasions.

13. That you consent to the landmark that no new Lodge can be formed without permission from the Grand Lodge, and that no countenance must be given to any irregular Lodge, or to any person clandestinely initiated therein, being contrary to the Ancient Charges of the Order.†

---

* A proper notice is equivalent to " a due summons" spoken of in subsequent pages. It must be in writing, signed by the Secretary, and authenticated by the Lodge seal.

† Referring to the well-known passages in the Ancient Charges.

14. That you consent to the landmark that no person can be regularly made a Mason in or admitted a member of any regular Lodge without previous notice, and due inquiry into his character.

15. That no visitors shall be received into your Lodge without due examination, and producing proper vouchers of their having been initiated in a regular Lodge."

Having signified your cordial submission to these ancient regulations in the hearing of the Lodge (and perhaps a large and mixed audience besides,) as the regulations of Free and Accepted Masons, as Masters in all ages have done before you, the most important emblems of Masonry were then placed in your hands and moralized upon, that the scope and purpose of Masonry being explained to you, you might not hereafter plead ignorance of them. These were:

1. *The Holy Writings.*—They were declared to be THE GREAT LIGHT IN MASONRY, which will guide you to all truth, will direct your path to the temple of happiness, and point out to you the whole duty of man.

2. *The Square.*—This teaches you to regulate your actions by rule and line, and to harmonize your conduct by the principles of morality and virtue.

3. *The Compass.*—This teaches you to limit your desires in every station, that rising to eminence by merit, you may live respected and die regretted.

4. *The Rule.*—This directs you punctually to observe your duty, to press forward in the path of virtue, and, neither

inclining to the right or left in all your actions, to have eternity in view.

5. *The Line.*—This teaches you the criterion of moral rectitude, to avoid dissimulation in conversation and action, and to direct your steps to the path which leads to immortality.

6. *The Book of Constitutions.*—This you were commanded to search at all times, and to cause to be read in your Lodge, that none may pretend ignorance of the excellent precepts it enjoins *

7. *The By-laws of your Lodge.*—These you were directed to see carefully and punctually executed.

These grand, and even sublime lessons, being thus publicly urged upon your official acceptance, you are henceforth bound to observe them, and enforce them upon your Lodge. You can not honorably say that you " did not *in words* agree to them, and therefore it is optionary upon you whether or not you will obey them." This were but a shallow equivocation. They were before your eyes in all the published works of Masonry. They were delivered to you in the public audience of your Lodge, and the world, and by every principle of honor you are covenanted to stand to and abide by them during your term of office.†

---

* See a correct copy of the *Book of Constitutions.*

† Upon this principle, the Master of a Lodge who denies the binding force of the Holy Writings as divinely inculcated, violates his solemn covenants of installation, and is subject to removal from office.

That you might be properly supported in your dignity as Master, the officers of your Lodge were next covenanted and installed by yourself, each in his peculiar station, and their chief duties pointed out and enforced upon them. The Wardens were commanded to assist you in the discharge of your trust. The Secretary was informed that he was to ob serve your will and pleasure (Monitor, p. 92); the Deacons that it was their province to attend upon you. Following this, you were emphatically assured that "the honor, reputation, and usefulness of your Lodge would materially depend upon the skill and assiduity with which you managed its concerns, and that the happiness of your fellow members would be generally promoted in proportion to the zeal and ability with which you should propagate the genuine principles of the institution." As a pattern of imitation, the most appropriate to your new office, your attention was directed to the SUN, the great luminary of nature, which, rising in the East, regularly diffuses light and lustre to all within its circle. Thus you, *the Sun of your Lodge*, were exhorted to spread and communicate light and instruction thereto. You were directed forcibly to impress upon your brethren the dignity and high importance of Masonry; seriously to admonish them never to disgrace it; charge them to practice *out* of the Lodge the duties taught *in* it, and by amiable, discreet, and virtuous conduct convince mankind of the goodness of the institution. Finally, the brethren of the Lodge, one and all, were directed to *obey* you according to the old charges and regulations,

" with all humility, reverence, love, and alacrity," and so the work, government, discipline, and instruction of your Lodge were left confidingly in your charge.

In a softened spirit you returned home that evening, to draw your designs upon your Trestle Board for the coming year. Fluttered and confused in your yet novel station, you look upon the charter of the Lodge which you have taken home with you* with a sensation of oppressiveness, and ask yourself, " What am I that I should bear this great trust ?" Opening those Holy Writings whose Masonic relations have been this day so forcibly brought to your mind, you read with a new and startling interest the words following:

"In Gibeon .the Lord appeared to Solomon in a dream by night: and God said, Ask what I shall give thee.

" And Solomon said, Thou hast showed unto thy servant David, my father, great mercy according as he walked before thee in truth and in righteousness, and in uprightness of heart with thee; and thou has kept for him this great kindness that thou hast given him a son to sit on his throne, as it is this day.

" And now, oh Lord my God, thou hast made thy servant king, instead of David, my father, and *I am but a little child : I know not how to go out or to come in.*

---

* The Charter is in the Master's keeping, and he is responsible to the Grand Lodge for its safety as custodian. He should have it rolled and preserved in a tin case (not framed) and either carry it home with him, or place it in the Secretary's charge, to be carefully locked up and delivered only to him or his order, or in his absence, to the Wardens.

" And thy servant is in the midst of thy people, which thou hast chosen a great people, that cannot be numbered nor counted for multitude.

" *Give therefore thy servant an understanding heart to judge thy people, that I may discern between good and bad :* for who is able to judge this, thy so great a people ?"—1st Kings, III. 5-9.

Pausing here to make personal application of these beautiful passages, your mind involuntarily soars upward upon the same wings that bore the soul of the youthful Grand Master to the Throne of Grace, and you beseech the Supreme Architect as he did, for "an understanding heart to judge the brethren under your government, that you may discern between good and bad." Solemnized by an appeal which the ever-present Deity will surely hear and answer, you pursue the passage to its conclusion, and read thus :

" And the speech pleased the Lord that Solomon had asked this thing.

" And God said unto him, Because thou hast asked this thing—hast asked for thyself understanding to discern judgment, behold I have done according to thy words ! Lo, I have given thee a wise and understanding heart ; so that there was none like thee before thee, neither after thee shall any rise like unto thee.

" And if thou wilt walk in my ways to keep my statutes and judgments, *then I will lengthen thy days.*"

There is nothing needed beyond this. You *accept the promise, having made the covenant,* and henceforth your hopes of usefulness, your reasonable anticipations of an extension of the office in your hands, and your expectations of an honorable and happy term of employment are *laid upon God.*

Now you draw your designs upon your trestle-board for the ensuing year. Now you note down your wishes and determinations—perhaps they assume this form.

1. That I will perform all my official duties as between myself and my conscience, being guided therein by my Installation Covenants.

2. That I will rule my Lodge without fear, favor, or hope of reward, save the approbation of my conscience and of God.

3. That I will endeavor to win my brethren to attend all the meetings of the Lodge by the allurements of abundant Masonic instruction for their wages.

4. That I will at all times, and by all means, seek for the ancient Work and Lectures of Masonry, and be satisfied with nothing less.

5. That the distressed worthy brother shall never go disappointed from the door of my Lodge, if in my power to aid him.

6. That I will strive, in knowledge, charity, truth, courtesy, and love, to be a model to my brethren.

7. That the evil-doer under my jurisdiction shall have no rest until he reforms or is cut off.

8 That the officers under me shall each acquire and perform his duties accurately and thoroughly, according to his Installation Covenants.

9. That my Lodge shall have honor and respect among its fellows.

A brief view of the work before you will end this chapter.

You have indeed got much to do. Not only have you the

current duties of your office to perform, which are likely, by the way, to require as much of your time as you can well spare from your necessary vocations; but there is probably much unfinished business lying over from last year, which must be cleared up before you can have the records and current management of the Lodge fairly in your hands. Odds and ends it is; fragments of disciplinary cases long spun out by special pleading, absence, or neglect; Committees failing to report from month to month; financial statements and misstatements that do not "balance" or "add up" properly; G. Secretary's communications; G. Lodge reports; volumes missing from the library; "blot minutes" missing and never entered upon the records; dues and collections frightfully behind; needed furniture, or equipments, etc., etc., and all demanding attention more or less prompt at your hands. To read up last year's records is, of course, the first thing you will do. And this suggests the propriety of making an abstract, as you read, of all unfinished business recorded there. To study the By-laws of your Lodge, point by point, and with pen in hand, is an equally important duty. Note their defects, their errors of omission and commission, and resolve, at an early period, if necessary, to awaken the Lodge to a sense of the importance of their amendment and perfection by the best models extant. Until this is done, you know that the By-laws of your Lodge, where not grossly contrary to the ancient landmarks, are *your guide*, and you must see them carefully executed.

CHAPTER II.

GETTING INTO THE HARNESS.

But few Lodges in this country are furnished with the auxiliaries for good and pleasant work. Few have even those which are demanded by stern necessity. The mania for building halls, so prevalent among us, so far embarrasses the Lodge finances when indulged in, as to leave no surplus funds to buy even the most important Masonic paraphernalia. The naked walls, bare floors, empty pedestals, and scanty and mean jewels and regalia of our Lodges cry aloud against this desecration of Lodge benevolences. Better for your Lodge to meet in the shabbiest garret, at a merely nominal rent, than in the costliest hall, if at the expense of so much that is essential to good work. Better assemble on a high hill or in a low dale, on mountain summit or in cryptic seclusion, enjoying the necessary tools and emblems of architecture for use, than in a broad apartment wanting those things.

Upon looking around you, and arranging matters to your mind before setting out upon your year's work, begin at the *Tyler's room*. Has he the instrument of his office? chairs for the comfortable seating of visitors? hooks for hats, coats, etc.? Is there a little sliding panel in the Lodge doors to enable him to peep in and observe the Lodge doings? (if so, *fasten it up immediately.* Don't allow it to remain for a moment. Nail it up and paper it over, and expressly forbid its being re-opened!) Has he the means of locking or hooking the Lodge door on the outside? Is he comfortably situated in reference to light and warmth?

Look next into the preparation-room. Is there a press for garments? chairs? table? Has the door to the Tyler's room the means of being fastened upon the inside?

Now enter the hall. Look at the paraphernalia of the Deacons. Have they good and proper rods? jewels of a correct pattern? a square and a compass, independent of those upon the altar?

Observe the Secretary's desk and appliances. Has he a commodious desk? Has he a chest and drawers that will securely lock? are his record and account books strong and well-bound? Has he plenty of stationery? Has he upon his shelves the proceedings of your Grand Lodge from the organization of your Lodge to the present time? Are they bound in durable volumes? Has he a seal, and a supply of blank demits, diplomas, accounts, etc.?

Note the Treasurer's desk. Observe his account book. Is it strong and durable? Has he stationery?

Look closely at the station of the Junior Warden. Has it a sheaf of wheat suspended over it? Has he a gavel of correct pattern, and a column, and a Monitor, and a candlestick? Is there a wall or pulpit before his chair? (If so, knock it down at once!) Has he a correct jewel of his office?

Observe the station of the Senior Warden. Has he the gavel, column, Monitor, and candlestick? Is there any obstruction before his chair? (Dash it down!) Has he a correct jewel of his office?

Give special attention to the Master's station. Has it the gavel, column, candlestick, Constitution and By-Laws? Has the carpenter pinned him in by a wall? (Take it away immediately!) Has he a correct jewel of his office?

Examine the floor of the Lodge room. Is it carpeted, or at least covered with some elastic substance that will deaden sound? Look at the walls. Is there the Master's Carpet for lecturing, and portraits of the great and good men who, through many ages, have adorned and made glorious the Order? Look at the seats provided for members and visitors. Are they abundant and comfortable? Is there a supply of water for drinking purposes? Is it neatly and cleanly distributed? Are the arrangements for warming the Lodge sufficient for comfort? Are the aprons abundant and clean? Are the By-Laws sufficient for all the members? Is the floor well swept?

Look now at the altar. Is it properly illuminated with the "Great and Lesser Lights?" Is the copy of Holy Scriptures one worthy of sacred use *in* the Lodge, and at public displays in processions *out* of it? Is the cushion upon which it rests a tasty one? Are the candlesticks what they should be? Is the altar itself such in form and size as it should be?

* * * * * * *

This examination into the furniture and paraphernalia of the

Lodge should precede your first meeting. It should be made with memorandum-book in hand, wherein you will notice whatever is defective or wanting. To supply *all deficiencies* will probably require your entire term of twelve months, perhaps longer, but to secure the most essential objects for Lodge use need not take you long. An incident here:

Brother C. A. F—— was elected Master of his Lodge in October, 1856. His Lodge, though ten years old, was as naked as a Caffre child is at the same age. But by the first regular communication of his Lodge, following his installation, Brother F. had secured a subscription paper from the community of which the following is a copy:

"Mrs. L. W.—A Bible cushion, very handsome.

"T. S. O., (a cabinet-maker)—A complete set of working tools, except the trowel, constructed of seasoned cherry wood, elegantly carved and adorned, with the donor's name and the name of the Lodge neatly engraved upon metal plates inserted in them.

"L. T., (a printer)—A new edition of the By-Laws, printed for one-fifth the regular price.

"W. W. A., (Bible Society Agent)—A large and noble copy of Scriptures.

"S. P. P., (a carpenter)—Four days work, raising and ornamenting the Lodge stations and pedestals, and repairing preparation-room.

"John Sherer—A Master's Carpet, large size.

"The young ladies of the *Sociable Sewing Club*—Cutting, trimming, and making forty aprons.

"J. B. E., (a jeweler)—Mending, altering, and polishing the jewels.

"N. R. T., (a bookseller)—Four quires paper, one quart ink, and a six quire blank book."

This subscription paper, worth perhaps in the aggregate $60, was made by Brother F., as he assured us, *within six days*, and the articles handed in, and the work engaged all done. The objects when displayed in the Lodge room, added so much to its beauty, gave the brethren such pleasure in the work and lectures, and so stimulated the zeal of the members, that an appropriation of $80 was speedily made, (followed in five months by $50 more), for the remaining paraphernalia, and to this day Bro. F.'s Lodge is the most comfortable and showy one in the District.

We relate this incident as a matter of encouragement. Our experience of Masons—no light one—assures us of their cheerful willingness to contribute to anything that promises to contribute to the honor and reputation of the craft, or the neatness, beauty, and facility of Masonic work. In David's preparations for the erection of the Temple, his people largely assisted. Upon his solicitation (1 Chronicles xxix) "they offered willingly, and gave for the service of the house of God, of gold 5,000 talents and 10,000 drams, and of silver 10,000 talents, and of brass 18,000 talents, and 100,000 talents of iron. And they, with whom precious stones were found, gave them to the treasure of the house of the Lord. Then the people rejoiced, for that they offered willingly, because with perfect heart they offered willingly to the Lord." Shall such experience as this be lost? Cheerful and abundant gifts can be secured from your brethren, if you will approach them right, and your naked and unfurnished Lodge will be made to smile under their bountiful benefactions. This, too, will prove the truth of the divine adage, " It is more blessed to give than to receive."

We have in a preceding sentence stigmatized the passion of erecting Masonic halls in this country as *insane.* Experience proves it to be so. The erection of Masonic halls in this country has so often proved the destruction of the Lodge by the crushing weight of the debts incurred, that we have learned to look upon Masonic halls, as we pass them in our journey, as so many cocoons which the silk-worm barely spins, *then dies.* Not one Lodge in ten ever has sufficient means to build a hall, nor in one case in twenty is there a necessity for it. Every village has some edifice with an upper apartment suitable, with a moderate fitting up, for Masonic purposes, and this should be secured before organizing the Lodge. The proposal to erect a hall usually comes from some property-holder in the place, or from some one who desires a business house or church edifice, and seeks Masonic aid for personal motives. ·You will do well during your term of office to pre-serve your Lodge from this temptation, *a mania for building.*

The necessity for a collection of the proceedings of your Grand Lodge is too apparent to mention. Have the Secretaries of your Lodge, during their respective terms of office, preserved those documents? Most probably not. It is by far more likely that there is not one of all the series on the shelves of the Lodge. A part may be found scattered amongst the dwellings of the members,—the most have gone to light the Tyler's fires, or the pipes and cigars of the brethren. In a sample Lodge, organized in 1818, not a single document or pamphlet, of all that have been provided (three copies are furnished per year) for forty-three years was to be found when the Master thereof was installed. How valuable would the collection be—had it been preserved—of the Proceedings, Constitutions, Addresses Circulars, By-Laws, College Reports, Funeral Notices, etc., etc., for forty-eight years ! How irreparable the loss!

If your search eventuates, as it probably will, in finding but a few straggling members of the series, and your study of Grand Lodge legislation, so necessary to the successful performance of your official duties is thereby seriously impeded, you may write to the Grand Secretary, asking for such copies as he can spare ; also institute a search among the book-shelves of your members, and address letters to the Lodges of your State. By these methods you may in time secure a considerable portion of the series. Let it be distinctly understood that, hereafter, all Grand Lodge and other documents furnished the Lodge in its official capacity *are the property of the Lodge*, and not to be taken out of the room until filed, bound, catalogued and numbered.

One difficulty you may expect to meet with at the outset of your administration—and in a lesser degree all through the twelve months—to which we will make special allusion here !

It is the prevalent notion in every Lodge (equally so in the Grand Lodge) *that the usages of that Lodge are necessarily correct.* The cry of " Oh, we don't work that way here !" which has chilled and paralyzed the intelligence and zeal of so many Masters, should have no terrors for you. · The idea that the particular customs of a Lodge are necessarily landmarks, is most preposterous and absurd. Upon this principle, Masonry *has no universal landmarks.* Every Lodge has customs peculiar to itself, customs that originated in temporary or local convenience or in official ignorance, customs which have been perpetuated through the ignorance, indifference, or timidity of subsequent Masters, and if these are to be esteemed as *landmarks*, there is no universality in Masonry. You who accepted as your first rule of private guidance, that " You will perform all your official duties as *between yourself and your conscience,* being guided therein by your installation covenants," must early learn to draw the line between local usage and universal landmarks, and must apply this to every step of the Lodge's progress during your official career.

At the same time you need not too abruptly change or cause to be changed the local practices of your Lodge. There is a soft and graceful method, a *suaviter in modo*, which is preferable to all others. Learn to use it. Go to each officer individually, and privately point out his errors, showing him at the same time the correct practice. The following directions in Scott's *System of Military Tactics*, are closely applicable to Masonic instruction, viz: " The instructor will always explain first what he proposes to teach, in a few clear and precise words. He will himself execute what he is about to command, by way of illustration, and endeavor to accustom the recruit, himself, to take the right position."

It may be that this wholesale course of innovation upon the Lodge usages will be so distasteful to the brethren as to excite murmurings, and even opposition. While there is but little danger of this, provided sufficient prudence and judgment upon your part are exercised, yet should it so happen, you must meet the difficulty in due time, and refer the question to the Grand Master. That dignitary is supposed to be well-instructed in general usage and Masonic landmarks. A statement of the question, lucidly drawn up, and accepted by both parties as ingenuous, should be forwarded to him, and his decision adopted without hesitation. If against you, you must submit, and ought to do it cheefully. If his decision is palpably wrong, (for even Grand Masters are *not* invariably Solomons,) you may lay the point before the Grand Lodge at a proper time.

We, however, repeat there is little danger of rebellion in the Lodge if the Master will but execute his great powers with prudence and rule without haughtiness or tyranny. Some of the members, especially the elder ones, may withdraw for a while from their attendance ; whisperings may be heard of a change of officers at the next election, etc., but if you will pursue a mild, yet firm and straight-forward course, according to the designs on your Trestle Board, described in Chapter

First, you will find, ere your year expires, that your fellow-members have forgotten their dislike to your *little* changes in their admiration at the successful and brilliant results. *The surest method of electioneering for re-election to office is to fill worthily that office while you have it.*

The financial matters of your Lodge, which are probably much confused, should have early attention. The first meeting of the Lodge should be primarily devoted to this subject. A list of debts and claims *due the Lodge*, and another of those due *by the Lodge*, should have been placed in your hands by the Secretary; if not, then order one promptly made out by the present incumbent. Get an order passed to print some blank accounts of dues, and direct the Secretary (whose duty it is "to observe the Worshipful Master's will and pleasure,") *to make out each brother's account and present it to him.* Get another order of the Lodge to pay all claims so far as audited and allowed, and draw orders upon the Treasurer accordingly. Give the Treasurer special orders never, *under any circumstances*, to pay out money without an order from you. Give the Secretary special orders as follows:

1. To enter upon the Records of the Lodge at each meeting the accounts of money received by him since the last regular meeting, and from whom.

2. To pay all moneys so collected over to the Treasurer before the close of the next regular meeting.

3. To take the Treasurer's receipts *as his only vouchers*.

4. To post from the Record Book to the Ledger every sum

so collected, carefully crediting it to the proper person, with dates and circumstances.

5. To pay no money, *under any circumstances*, save to the Treasurer.

To assure yourself of the Secretary's obedience, examine his books, specially the Record Book and Ledger, from time to time, and if erroneous, insist upon rigid corrections and more perfect attention to duty in future.

So important do we deem this subject that we boldly affirm that you will make no sound progress in your efforts to instruct, enlighten, and elevate your Lodge, until the financial arrearages are cleared away. Those who are largely in debt to the Lodge will shirk its meetings lest they should be reminded of their defalcations. Those who pay their dues punctually will be soured by the reflection that the burdens of the Lodge, which ought to be equally distributed amongst the entire membership, are made to fall upon the shoulders of a few. Objects of charity cannot be relieved, or necessary paraphernalia purchased, because the means of the Lodge are scattered in the pockets of non-paying members. If, therefore, you need three, or even six months, to roll this monstrous obstacle away; if various members must be suspended for non-payment of dues; if a portion of the just claims of the Lodge must be remitted and excused to the defaulters, look upon it as a necessary evil and rid yourself of the embarrassments, being assured of a clearer sky when it is done.

Nothing will tend more to your own encouragement and improvement than to open and maintain a private diary. Your first entries, after the personal determinations and programme described in Chapter First, will of course relate to the deficiencies in regalia, furniture, etc., etc., alluded to above. Your after entries will describe the obstacles met; the triumphs and the failures; the encouragements and discouragements; the letters written and received; the time devoted to study: the number of degrees conferred and upon whom; the visitations made and received; the personal expenses incurred by your Masonic labors; in short, the incidents of your official year. Such a diary, properly kept, is a document of permanent and immense value, not only to yourself, but to all with whom you sustain the fraternal relation. We shall find a place in a subsequent chapter to make extracts from existing records of this kind. That intelligent Craftsman, Grand Master Austin, of New Albany, Indiana, is one who originated and has sustained a private journal of the sort which in the days to come will approve itself to the pleasure and profit of his successors.

CHAPTER III.

OPENING AND CLOSING THE LODGE.

The ability of the true Lodge-Master is seen more in his style of *Opening* and *Closing* his Lodge than in any other department of official labor. It is the *experimentum crucis* of a good Master.

We have traveled long and far to see and hear what is this thing called *Masonry*. We have visited Lodges by scores of hundreds. We have learned that the expression "a good Lodge," chiefly means " a Lodge with a good Master," and we have learned that the test of a good Master is as stated above, his ability with dignity and accuracy to open and close his Lodge.

Some make the test "the ability to confer the Degrees." They are wrong. A Degree is not so much conferred by the Master as by the Senior Deacon and other officers. The attention of the Lodge is not then so much turned upon the Master as upon the Candidate. But in the ceremonies of *Opening* and *Closing*, the Master is the be-all and do-all of the Lodge.

In our remarks under this head, we take it for granted that the reader has familiarized himself with the thoughts given in preceding chapters. Basing our observations upon them, we go on to say that the Model Master should make his appearance at the Lodge room at least a quarter of an hour prior to the time of Opening specified in the By-laws. This is to see that all matters are in readiness for the meeting—for Tylers and Stewards need looking after as well as other folks; likewise to provide *pro tempore* appointments to offices whose proper incumbents are absent. This must not be left, as is too customary, until the last minute. If a Brother is to be called upon to fill a station, he *should know it* in season, and *should accept it.* This avoids the annoyance and mortification of refusal or failure. Again, there may be, and it is always to be presumed there *will be*, visitors in attendance. These, if properly instructed, are also at the Lodge room a quarter or half hour before the time of opening, which is specified in the By-laws. And these should promptly receive the cordial word and gentlemanly greeting which a Model-Master knows so well to bestow. These also, if strangers to the Brethren, should be put in charge of Committees of Examination in due time— *before the Lodge opens* if possible—so as to avoid that great annoyance so commonly inflicted upon Lodges, that of calling out the best of the members during the hours of business for the purpose of Examination. This indeed is an insufferable annoyance and an immense loss of Masonic time to those who are so unfortunate as to have it to do.

Precisely at the moment specified in the By-laws, the Master should Congregate his Lodge. If, after he has done so, there is not present a sufficient number for Opening, it will be optionary with the Master whether to wait a while for the others or dismiss those who are present and go home. The latter method was tried, once, by a sharp set young Master just installed, whose Lodge had become in the preceding years inveterately tardy. At the first meeting he Congregated his Lodge according to the By-laws, then, there being but five present, dismissed them, put the Charter in his pocket and went home. He summoned the Lodge to a called meeting the week following, explained the matter, showed the evils of tardiness and so worked up the impulses of the occasion as to have no more difficulty in that way the rest of the year ! The true theory is that the Lodge in its By-laws *sets the moment of opening*, and the Master at his Installation solemnly covenants himself to see those By-laws carefully and *punctually* executed. If the Lodge does not approve of the hour of meeting named in the By-laws, because it is too early or too late, let them change the By-laws : but while they are in force the Master should see them rigidly enforced, so far as he has the power to do it.

The Lodge being Congregated by the method which is or ought to be understood by every Master, the ceremonies of Purging and Tyling follow. The *method* of doing these cannot be explicitly described ; but many hints drawn from the MODEL MASTER of this century* can be given. He intimates

---

* Alluding of course to Brother Thomas Smith Webb, whose death in 1819 opened the way to the deluge of innovations that have swept over the Lodges. Those who had the

that the peculiar study of every Mason present ought to be to have the ceremony of opening the Lodge conducted with propriety. That to the rulers of the Lodge every eye is turned for propriety of conduct and behavior. That no one present at the opening can be exempt in taking a share in the ceremony; it being a general concern, all must assist.* That we must detect impostors among those present if any, and that due care must be directed to the external avenues of the Lodge. He observes that three purposes are wisely effected in this manner of opening the Lodge, viz.: the Master is reminded of the dignity of his character, and the Brethren of the homage and veneration which are due from them, † while a reverential awe for the Deity is inculcated and the eye is fixed on that object from whose radiant beams LIGHT only can be derived. ‡ Thus we are taught to adore the God of Heaven and to supplicate his protection in our well-meant endeavors. Then

---

happiness to sit under his instructions testify to the dignity, urbanity, skill and power with which he ever wielded the Gavel whether on the quiet dais of his own Lodge or in the Grand East of the Grand Lodge. He was in all respects, with tongue and pen and gavel, the MODEL MASTER of the XIXth Century, as William Preston was of the XVIIIth.

* This includes the Secretary as well as the others. The claim that the Secretary has his minutes to keep up, and therefore cannot rise and act with the rest is untenable and absurd.

† This idea of veneration is from the following in the Ancient Charges: "The rulers and governors of the Lodge are to be obeyed in their respective stations by all the Brethren with all humility, reverence, love and alacrity."

‡ Alluding of course to the Holy Scriptures.

him his Wardens who accept their trust after the customary salutations. And that the Brethren then with one accord unite in duty and respect, and so the ceremony concludes.

But while these hints point out plainly enough a proper skeleton of the ceremonies of Opening, detailed information upon particular passages may be added. The rules of Purging a Lodge are often grossly disregarded, either from neglect of the Rituals or ignorance of them. The true regulation is, that no one can be present when the secrets of Masonry are to be dispensed (as in Opening the Lodge, etc.,) except he has been found to be as just and lawful a Mason as we ourselves are who make up the Lodge. This fact must be ascertained by one of three methods, viz: 1, strict trial, 2, due examination or 3, lawful information. The Master is the judge of all this, and he alone is responsible that the regulation alluded to is observed. * "Trial" and Examination" are esoteric. They are rigidly defined and there is no " short way" by which they can be effected. No stranger, however expert, can pass through the ordeal of "strict trial and due examination," so as to enter the Lodge, in a less period than half an hour. Thousands with their present knowledge (or want of knowledge) could never pass them all. "Lawful Information" is exoteric. It consists in some Brother present *vouching* that

---

* See an excellent article under this head from the pen of Finlay M. King, now Grand Master of New York: first pub lished in *The Masonic Union.*

the Master assumes his government in due form and under " he knows the visitor to be a Mason" by one of the kinds of knowledge named in the regulation above given. A may vouch for B if he has set with him in a Lodge opened on the Degree in question, or A may vouch for B, if C has previously vouched to A for B. There is the whole in a nutshell.

The Lodge being Congregated, Purged and Tyled, is now Lectured by the Master in catechetical form with the aid of the Senior Warden or any other Brother whom the Master may prefer. The system is esoteric. It is rigidly defined; no Mason or Lodge or Grand Lodge has a right to vary a syllable or letter from it. It enlightens the members present in the very matters most necessary to a Mason; the government of his own conduct; his ties, bonds, chairs and covenants; the means of traveling as a Mason; the method of filling Masonic office creditably; the method of examining a visitor systematically; of conferring Degrees; of examining a candidate for advancement—all these and more are conveyed in the technical "Lecturing," necessary to be done at opening the Lodge.* The pledges of a Past Master can be fulfilled with nothing short of this.

The Religious Exercises at opening might well be extended beyond the usual practice of Masters. The reading of appropriate passages of Scripture; and the Singing a proper Ode

---

* To open the Lodge thoroughly *on the three Degrees* takes an expert Master from 25 to 35 minutes for the whole.

might well be added to the usual Prayer.   All the surroundings of a Masonic Lodge, being sympolical of a religious thought, this is a good time to evolve some of their lessons.

The *Reception of a Visitor* is a proper subject to come under this head.   We have already alluded to his examination as a rigid thing, a matter in which no favors should be asked and none can be given.   When we travel as Masons we travel upon our " rights, lights and benefits."   We ask to *receive ;* if we ask properly we have a right to receive.*   We claim to see the Charter, the By-Laws and the List of members.   The Lodge then claims the " strict trial" to which we have alluded.   This we concede, but we claim that they ask the proper questions in precise language and order.   We reply in proper language and order.   All being done, the Examining Committee returns to the Lodge, reports the character of our examination, names our mistakes if any and is discharged.   The Master then decides upon our admission or rejection and there is no appeal.

If admitted the visitor is met at the door by the proper officer (the Senior Deacon) who introduces himself, and is introduced by him to the Master.   The Master then introduces him to the Lodge and gives him the appropriate welcome. How precious is this to its recipient ! how rarely is it properly done !   The visitor, but a moment before " a stranger in a

---

* Unless some Brother present objects to our admission.   In this case his "rights" are paramount to ours.

strange land"—sternly questioned—refused all reply to *his* questions, left alone while the Committee report whether he is to be treated as an enlightened or a benighted man, is now the "observed of all observers,"—the welcomed—the friend— the Brother. Smiling faces, grasping hands, loving words are his, and his by *right*. *This is the wages of Masonry.* Now he finds that Masonry is all it claims to be, and he feels to thank God that he ever entered its portals. He will remember that reception and that Lodge so long as he lives.

But all this depends upon the Master. Defects in him are irremediable. If he is awkward, if he is surly, if he is igno- rant, it is all at the expense of the visitors, it is so much to be deducted from his wages as a Mason. It is to the discredit of the Lodge, of the Grand Lodge, of the Masonic Order; and the visitor will only remember that reception as one more proof how far Masonry has fallen below its ancient standard.

The Master of every Lodge is supposed to be in regular line of advancement to be Grand Master. He should practice all the grace, dignity and wisdom in the use of the wooden gavel that will be expected of him when he handles the ivory one. The same general principles apply to the opening of the Grand Lodge as the subordinate. Had we more knowledge and dig- nity in Masters we should be less frequently mortified by the want of both in Grand Masters. But we forbear.

As one great object had in view by every Brother in attend- ing his Lodge is " to improve himself in Masonry," we advise by all means that at each Regular Meeting the Lodges be opened in order on three Degrees, beginning with the lowest. It only takes half an hour to do all this and the effect of it will be most happy. Entered apprentices will attend the Lodge so that they may see the Lodge opened in form. Fellow Crafts will do the same. To confine the opening to the Third Degree is to restrict within the narrowest compass the dissemination of light to the Lodge.

As we have so urgently recommended the Master to open the Lodge punctually at the moment indicated in the By-laws, so with the Closing. The By-laws may specify the time of closing; if they do not, endeavor to have them improved in that particular and then time the Work so as to shut down the gate upon it at the proper moment. Two hours well employed is ample time for a Lodge meeting. It is as long as the tired, the sick, the feeble and the active business men care to stay. It is as long as the common mind will drink in instruction without weariness. If the work is unfinished, lay it over. If Degrees are to be conferred make Called Meetings for them; but avoid the frequent error of protracted meetings of the Lodge. It is not a bad rule, that given us by the venerable Father ——, now at rest under the pine trees. It was this: "If when you get home from the Lodge your wife scowls upon you, take it as the punishment for exceeding the By-Laws!"

CHAPTER IV.

DIGNITY AND TACT.

Dignity and Tact—Tact and Dignity, (we scarcely know which to put foremost,) are qualifications in a Master equal in importance to any others. For want of *Dignity*, many a Master fails just short of being a " Model ;" for want of *Tact*, many a Master experiences a total failure *maugre* Knowledge, Dignity and Zeal. To govern men, especially *free* men, men used to republican-democratic liberties, and unused to the despotic sort of control which is the very genius of Masonry, is a quality few possess by nature, and one, the acquisition of which compensates for almost any amount of study and effort.

Shall we draw two sketches, both from life, and both derived from the same Lodge ? The last was taken about five years later than the other. The Lodge shall be called " Experience Lodge," and the names of the two Masters A. and B. In our first visit to that Lodge A. was Master. We entered as a visitor and were received as one. The Master stepping forward to the front of the dais, with a grace and dignity that would have become a " a belted knight, a lord, a duke and a' that," gave us a welcome we can never forget. Looking round the hall, we saw his courtesy and grace reflected in every Brother present. Taking a seat by his side, we witnessed a scene of order and decorum only paralleled in the Supreme Court at Washington. When a Brother rose to speak, he felt that he was protected by the head of the Lodge ; that in fact he *was* the head of the Lodge, so long as he confined himself to the theme under discussion and kept himself circumscribed within the By-laws. When Bro. A. had occasion to put a member right—and the theme of discussion that night was one of deep interest, one in which feelings were involved and character was at stake—he did it without the slightest compromise of good manners or the brotherly cement that bound all together. No jesting or levity was visible, and when each member had spoken at pleasure, the subject was impressively summed up and committed to the decision of the Lodge.

And all this was done with much less real Masonic knowledge than should have been found in the Master. In fact Bro. A. was not a bright Mason either in rituals, jurisprudence or parliamentary law. Many of his conclusions would have failed " to hold water," as the saying is. But the air of sincerity— for he was sincere—and of dignity—for he did appreciate the dignity of his position as the Representative of King Solomon —made up for all deficiencies, and his official year has been considered more successful than that of any of his predecessors.

One thing, too, struck us very forcibly, viz., the manner in which at proper times he could unbend. At partaking of the refreshments which the Lodge had provided as part of our welcome, he was the life and soul of the party. "He came

down," as the old Tyler whispered it in our ear, "better from
his high stilts than any man you ever saw." He sang. He told
anecdotes. He was funny. Nay, we are not sure but what, if
a reporter had been present, he would needs have expunged
certain portions of his remarks ere committing them to print.
But when the call to labor was made, and the Master put on
his hat, the boldest of us would not have dared essay a smile
in his presence! Now that is what we call *Dignity in the
right place*. His fellow-members respected and obeyed him,
and unconsciously acquired and reflected a part of his manner
while in the Lodge. Plain country people, dressed in plain
country clothes, they looked absolutely intellectual as being
under the shadow of the Throne!

The same Brother A., while conducting cases of discipline
in his Lodge, was a very Rhadamanthus in manner, though
kind enough at the bottom. No special pleading could move
him from his rock, no insult, had any one dared offer it, could
have made him forget his dignity. He carried his gravity of
manner into the Grand Lodge, and it carried him from the
floor to the Deputy Grand Mastership, and thence, naturally
enough, to the Grand East. So much for our first picture.

The second one introduces Bro. B. A good, genial fellow
he was, and a hard student. He had been twice or thrice
Chairman of the Committee on Foreign Correspondence in
his Grand Lodge, a station which makes the *ready Mason*,
if any thing can. He had held office in the Grand Lodge,
where he was justly esteemed for his large heart and well filled

mind. But in our visit to his Lodge, we were simply disgusted with his want of Dignity. He sat with coat off and feet upon the table before him. He was "hail fellow, well met" with his Lodge, each member of which took every imaginable liberty with him, and at the same time despised him. The Lodge wilted under his mismanagement, and has never recovered its tone of former honor and respect.

In looking back upon our personal acquaintances, we believe that every Master whom we recollect for his successful handling of the Gavel, was a man of personal Dignity while in the East. The gentleman who presided at our own making was pre-eminently so. Charles Scott was remarkable for this. James Penn was a model of personal deportment. Wm. B. Hubbard is remembered by all who ever saw him preside for this valued quality.

If any special advice under this head is desired, we venture to lay down the following :

1. Never permit yourself to perpetrate a jest while in the East. The readiness with which a laugh can be excited by the Master is a dangerous temptation, and is to be carefully avoided.

2. Allow no infringement of decorum in the Lodge to pass by unnoticed and unrebuked. It is not always necessary that rebukes should be *public*, but they should be thorough. An occasional reading of the Ancient Charges under this head will be found suggestive, especially the following passages : "You are not to hold private committees or separate conver-

sation without leave from the Master, nor to talk of anythin
impertinent or unseemly, or interrupt the Master or Warden
or any Brother speaking to the Master; nor behave yourse
hilariously or jestingly while the Lodge is engaged in what
serious and solemn, nor use any unbecoming language upc
any pretense whatever, but to pay due reverence to you
Master."

3. In all your acts and words, consider yourself as represen
ing another and a nobler character. The Master is not electe
to be merely a Chairman or Presiding Officer of a society.
he were, it would be sufficient that he simply keep order an
push the business through. But he assumes a different nam
and character, becomes covenanted by new ties and assume
responsibilities to a different power (the Grand Lodge,) fro
his fellow members.

But it is much easier to describe Dignity than Tact. *Ta*
is defined to be "peculiar skill or faculty: nice perception c
discernment." It is the gift of *doing the right thing at the rigi
time*, and without it no Master can be eminently successfu
A Master of Tact rarely offends a fellow member, becaus
though his *decisions* may be adverse, his *manner* is so winnin;
his *words* so gentle that no rational offense can be taken
Formerly the By-laws of Lodges were not extended to embrac
"the Order of Business," for it was deemed proper to entru:
the time and distribution of business to the Tact of th
Master: this is but right, seeing that he alone is held respo
sible by the Grand Lodge. Such a Master will get throug

more business in an hour, and do it better than others without
this practical Tact, can in two, especially if embarrassed with
an "Order of Business," which is as much like business as the
Georgia mountaineer's method of carrying a rock in one end
of his meal-bag to balance the corn in the other end!

LET YOUR LIGHT SHINE.

"Let your light shine," the MASTER said,—
  "To bless benighted man!
The light and truth my Spirit shed
  Are yours to shed again."

We come, oh Lord, with willing mind,
  That knowledge to display;
Enlighten us, by nature blind,
  And glad we will obey.

CHAPTER V.

DISPENSING LIGHT AND KNOWLEDGE.

There is no subject to be treated of in the present series more important than this of "dispensing light and knowledge." It refers to the highest and noblest duty of a Master. It is a sacred charge twice alluded to in the *Installation Services of a Master.* " You are to propagate a knowledge of the Art. For a pattern of imitation, consider the great luminary of nature, which, rising in the East, regularly diffuses light and luster to all within its circle. In like manner it is your province to spread and communicate light and instruction to the Brethren of your Lodge." * It is the very salvation of Masonry, perpetuating it for the ages to come as it has been perpetuated from the ages past. It secures to each visitor to the Lodge "wages," ample to reward his coming. It vitalizes the entire body of the membership, calling out their good deeds of charity and fellowship. It is the all-in-all of Masonry. †

---

* *Miniature Monitor,* pp. 155 and 161. The general dissemination of this cheap and perfect copy of Webb's original Monitor, will do much to reduce the Master's labors in this direction.

† So the fathers one and all viewed it. Read some lines from one of the earlier editions of Webb's *Monitor,* in which the coming to Lodge " to hear Lectures" was given as the most laudable end a Mason could pursue.

In the programme which was suggested to you in the first Chapter of this series, you were suposed to make these resolutions: "That I will endeavor to allure my brethren to attend all the meetings of the Lodge by the allurements of abundant Masonic instruction for their wages."

"That I will at all times and by all means seek for *the ancient Work and Lectures of Masonry* and be satisfied with nothing less."—Now let us see how you can best fulfill these laudable purposes.

First.—Set yourself fixedly against all "short ways" of Opening Lodge, conferring Degrees, etc. This has become the blight of many Lodges: in seeking to economize a few minutes time all the essence and spirit of the ceremonials have been lost. It is as if the Christian minister, in dispensing the Holy Sacrament should content himself with distributing the bread and wine, omitting all explanations and applications of their meaning. It is as if, in the ceremony of baptism, the "short way" of dispensing with prayer and blessing were adopted. Set it down in your mind that when your Lodge assembles at a Regular Meeting it must invariably be opened with all ceremony and lecture. Symbolically Masons can only enter the Masonic Temple by entering the *Checkered Pavement,* and from thence to the *Middle Chamber*, and from thence to the *Sanctum Sanctorum.* To get into a Master's Lodge by any other method is historically absurd. * To open on the

* It recalls the comparison of Christ, wherein the robber is described as entering the sheepfold *over the wall;* the Shepherd of the sheep entering at the gate.

three Degrees in the proper way requires about a one-half hour's time for the three. Within that half hour is compressed a whole system of Masonry. Those who are present not only learn to open a Lodge, but to examine a candidate, to examine a visitor and to be examined when they journey from home. All this, however, has been described in the Third Chapter of this series and need not be recapitulated here.

That half hour regularly occupied in this way once a month from year to year is the very salt of the Lodge. It will in itself make the members "bright," even though they never have a Degree to confer, or a visitor to examine. * It is the "blessed half hour," as an old Mason styles it, "of Masonic light and knowledge."

In all your instructions as Master, confine yourself as rigidly *to manner* as to *matter*. That is, confine yourself to the catechetical system of instruction. Let all the technical knowledge you impart, (that is the knowledge of the Rituals,) be dispensed by *question and answer*. There is no other method so ancient, so easy, so natural or so successful. By this system you can always tell when you are right and the entire Lodge becomes a trained critic upon your performances. The old Masons used to number the questions and answers as children do while learning the catechism. The plan is followed in "The Miniature Monitor," which is coming into very general

---

* This term "bright" was originally employed as the highest compliment that could be paid a Mason.

use. Adopting this idea it would require fifty-five questions and answers to afford the necessary instruction in opening a Lodge of Entered Apprentices.

The practice of giving the Lectures in " narrative" form, which has fallen into considerable use, is in every point of view reprehensible. Not only is it a modern innovation, which is itself a suspicious fact, but in itself it is unphilosophical· It is a constant temptation to the instructor to interpolate his own words, and, by an easy transition, his own ideas. No man is a reliable Lecturer who adopts it. No man, in any half dozen repetitions, will follow the same course of language or thought. The method is at first adopted by some to avoid wearisome repetition ; by some to save time ; * by some to give themselves an opportunity to show off. Neither of these reasons is justifiable. It is recorded of the old Lecturers, Preston, Webb, Cross and Cushman, that they never, under any circumstances, varied in word from question or answer when lecturing upon the Rituals, and that they laid as much stress upon *manner* as *matter.* †

To avoid the monotony of which some complain as a result of the catechetical style of instruction, you can call more of the

---

* But it does *not* save time. Time is always best econo mized when system is most employed.

† Webb was in the habit of replying to those who asked for explanations, endeavoring to provoke an argument, " If you will commit to memory the Lectures, you will know as much as I do."

members of the Lodge into use to answer your questions. In the Monitor * it is forcibly said : " From a share in this ceremony (Opening Lodge) no Mason can be exempted. It is a general concern, in which all must assist. . . .The intent of the meeting becomes the sole object of attention, and the mind is insensibly drawn from those indiscriminate subjects of conversation which are apt to intrude on our less serious moments." We are aware that this exhortation does not so much apply to the catechism as to other matters ; yet by an easy transition, it may be applied to that with much propriety. Some of the best Masters we ever saw call, in the aid of the Brethren, one by one, until every Brother present has responded to one or more questions.

We will say further in relation to the " narrative" form of lecturing, that it is not so interesting to the Lodge as the catechetical form. For why do we rehearse the Lectures so frequently in the Lodge ? Is it to *interest* the members ? Surely not. They know them, that is the *meaning* of them, as well after a dozen rehearsals as they will ever know them. But they listen to them over and over again, from month to month, and from year to year, that they may eventually *commit them to memory*, so that they may in turn repeat them when they travel from home, and may be competent to teach them to the newly-made Brethren in their own Lodge, and may be able, if

---

* *Miniature Monitor*, p. 20.

placed in official seats, to rehearse them to the Lodge or Grand Lodge. To secure these advantages, the *catechetical form* must be pursued; the questions as well as the answers must be given. And here let us say from our own experience, that to learn to *ask* the questions in the proper language and in their proper order, is at least twice as difficult as to learn to answer them when asked. * This is an additional argument in favor of frequent repetitions of the questions. In the Schools of Instruction which have recently been held with such success in various States, many of the delegates who had fallen into the pernicious habit of the "narrative" style, just mentioned, became convinced of their error, and it was the unanimous resolve of the multitudes who participated in those Schools, to abandon it and adhere strictly to the old method.

In dispensing light and knowledge through the Rituals, we advise you to do it without the use of a Monitor. Commit to memory every word of the Monitorial passages, out of the Lodge, so that they will dovetail into the esoteric passages and be heard by your auditory without the change of voice so common and so destructive to the continuity of the passages. One great credit at least is due to our Pennsylvania Brethren, and they take great credit for it ; that you rarely see a Mon-

---

* A visitor has as much right to refuse to answer questions not in the Ritual, as you have to refuse his admission should he fail to answer those that *are* in the Ritual.

itor in their Lodge-rooms. If one of their Masters cannot give the necessary instruction without referring to the book, he calls upon some one who can. This rule is borrowed from England where, Bro. E. D. Cooke informs us, you never see any book in the Lodge-room, save the By-Laws. We have many Masons equally skilled; some even who can repeat from memory the entire Funeral and installation services. * After all, this is but little more matter than every theatrical performer is required to commit to memory every week. Every school boy in an advanced class does as much every month ; and surely the Master, the "Model" Master, who desires to honor himself, his Lodge and the Craft at large, is impelled by an ambition as noble as that of the histrionic performer or the .sclool boy !

The difference between that style of instruction which seems to be extemporaneous,—which seems to come from the heart,—in which the Master looks into the eyes of the candidate and repeats to him the elegant and forcible passages upon Masonic morality, science and religion,—and that other style in which the Master holds a book in one hand and a candle in the other, and endeavors through moist and smoky spectacles to read the same passages to him, is too great to need illustration. Who has listened to a dull Senior Deacon plodding

---

* Bro F. N. Porter—we name him with a sigh—had acquired this practice, much to the effectiveness of his course as a Lecturer.

through the Second Section of the Fellow-Craft, without mentally wishing the prosy utterances would come to an end? Yet the same thing, repeated as if from the impulse of the moment, is not wearisome.

Having said so much of the importance of exact Ritual teaching, we now proceed to answer the query: But is there no scope for the Master to expatiate upon these things? Has he no field for the display of his historical studies, his explorations into moral science, in Bible topics? Must he confine himself to the mere role of a parrot and utter passages by rote until his soul become weary? Our reply is, *there is a boundless scope for a wise and intelligent Master.* It lies in his explaining and illustrating the text. His part is that of the exact Minister who, taking care to quote the language of Scripture with verbal accuracy, brings all his knowledge of science and literature into play to illustrate and explain it. There is no limit, no boundary to the Master's privilege of explanation. All we ask of him is, *that he quote the text correctly.* The sermon is his own affair.

And how much may be said in the way of illustration to the delight and instruction of a Lodge, is known only to those who have enjoyed the rare privilege of an intelligent Master. We have in our mind's eye one, not old in Masonry or in years, yet whose mind is so stored with sound reading that upon a single Masonic text, he pours forth a volume of matter, "new and old." With whom every Scripture passage illustrates a passage of Masonic text. With whom every point of moral philosophy, every fact from the Historians of olden time, every discovery among the ruins of the past, has its Masonic signification, and to whom all the teachings of Masonry are but so many incentives to higher flights in celestial lore.* True it is not given to every Lodge to have a ———, yet every Master may derive from his general reading a flood of knowledge bearing upon and explanatory of the Ritual. His Botany will inform him what plant is the Acacia. His Geography wil enlighten him as to the location of Joppa and Tyre and Jerusalem. His Mineralogy will explain the term " Parian marble." His Architecture will elucidate a thousand questions referable to King Solomon's Temple. His English Dictionary will enable him to pronounce correctly those words, (" piques," " architect," etc.,) which are so apt to come in wrong shape from the East. His Bible, Josephus, Herodotus, etc., will make him in many things a full and a bright Mason.

We recommend the practice of monthly essays on Masonic themes, to be prepared by the Master and such brethren as he may select. These should be very brief—in no case occupying more than ten or fifteen minutes, and entirely practical. The conventional bore of the " Morality of Masonry," should be avoided and practical information substituted. These essays after being read should be filed in the archives of the Lodge as objects of value.

---

* Some who do not know J. Aug. Williams, LL. D., of Harrodsburg, Ky., may need to be told to whom we refer.

A considerable part of the instruction due the Lodge from the Master lies in the reading and expounding the Proceed⁻ ing of the Grand Lodge. This is unquestionably a covenanted duty, though so rarely attended to. And here let us remark that the printed documents sent out by the Grand Lodge are not the property of the Master and Wardens, as seems to be generally supposed, but of the Lodge. They are a part of the literary treasures of the Lodge. They should be preserved, bound up into volumes, made practical by indexes, numbered and laid up for the use of the Lodge. In the course of years they become invaluable. It is your duty, as soon as the Pro⁻ ceedings of the Grand Lodge come to hand, to read them from meeting to meeting, to expound them by the light of previous legislation and at once to put in force the edicts and requisi- tions they may contain.

As a means of instruction, the readiest and most practical at your hand, we advise you early in your official career to organ⁻ ize a *School of Instruction* in your Lodge. This needs no War- rant or authority from the Grand Lodge, but is within the scope of the Master's prerogatives: nay, of any individual Mason. The most practical plan of a School of Instruction extant is found in a form of By Laws and Instructions pub· lished in 1861, in Indiana. The peculiarity of the plan lies chiefly in making the teacher a movable officer, and a proxy and guide to all. The system recognizes six officers, of whom one serves for Tyler and Janitor, one for the Deacons, one for Secretary and Treasurer, one to fill the East, and one for each of the Warden's Stations. The real Conductor is the second named above: he is the general prompter and executive. The system requires that changes in the various parts be so frequently made that every member of the School shall be called upon at every Meeting to take some part and give some response. The preamble of these By-Laws explains the purposes of a School in these words: "To enlighten the minds of the Fraternity in this vicinity in the knowledge of the sublime ceremonies and instructions of the mystic art of Masonry, and to improve our hearts under the Divine influence of Brotherly Love, Relief and truth, Temperance, Fortitude, Prudence and Justice, we have united ourselves into a Masonic School of Instruction and do agree to be bound by the following By-Laws and Rules of Order during our connection therewith."

At each meeting of such a School there are eight departments of business to be attended to:

1.   The Exemplification of Examining a Visitor.

2·   The Exemplification of Opening a Lodge on some one Degree.

3.   The Rehearsal of the three Altar Charges.

4.   The Exemplification of the Winding Stairs.

5.   The Rehearsal of the Funeral Oration.

6.   Miscellaneous Business.

7.   The Exemplification of Calling off and Calling on a Lodge in one Degree.

8. The Exemplification of Closing a Lodge on some one Degree.

Exactly two hours are consumed in these exercises, and the results of such a School, regularly maintained for a few months, may be summoned up in these words which we quote ; " Every Member of this School can examine a Visitor; every Member can stand an Examination; every Member ean Examine a Candidate ; every Member can open and close the Lodge." But if only one result were attained, if only each officer of the Lodge would learn his duty and response, it were well worth the time and trouble of maintaining the School for a few months.

The beauty and sublimity of the Masonic Drama are such as to arouse the desire of excellence in its exhibition to the highest pitch. There is nothing outside the lids of the Bible so grand, solemn, sublime, as the Dramatic lessons that make up the life of a Mason from his first alarm at the Northwest corner of the Lodge to the moment the " clods of the valley" and the " green sprigs of the grove" are dropped upon his coffin. There is a perfect sequence to each ceremony explaining the last and suggesting the next ; there is a practical thought in each symbol gaveling the whole harmony together. All point to higher attainments in the present life, and trust in God for the life to come. All suggest kindness to our fellow man as the best means of pleasing God ; and of pleasing God as the highest source of human happiness. Is not the post of Hierophant of these mysteries then a noble one ? Is there not enough to reward the ambition of the most learned and intelligent man in the thought that by due study and practice he may worthily display these mysteries to his fellows?

There is yet another sort of "light and knowledge" which it is the duty of the Master to dispense. We allude to *out-door* instruction. The *Monitor* provides for a course of teaching to the *world without.* This is conveyed in the form of public Installations, of Corner-Stone Deposits, Dedications of Halls and Public Edifices, and the Burial of the Dead. How often these impressive forms are made nought in the sight of the people, we need not say. We feel assured that as a whole, Masonry is more damaged than benefited by them; that more people are deterred from uniting with us than allured, by what they see of our ceremonies. But this is not attributable to any defect in the ceremony, but in the conductor of the ceremony. Let it be your charge, oh, Model Master, when you lead forth a band of Masons from the tyled precincts of the Lodge, to display the beauty and grace of Masonic symbolisms to an admiring world. Be yourself thoroughly instructed in the meaning of these public displays. They are designed to remove prejudices, to conquer opponents, to call out friends. They are the very seed of the future Lodge. The boys and young men who gaze upon them are those who are to handle the mystic implements after we are dead. The females whose acute eye watch your proceedings, are the future mothers of those who will build up or pull down your Lodge. It has been said, "that one good Mason properly interred brings forth twelve to the future honor of the Lodge." We have seen a corner-stone properly planted by less than thirty Masons, produce twice thirty before the hall was ready for dedication.

And, finally for this chapter, bear in mind that the best and only lawful means of electioneering for the next election to the Mastership and to the Grand Mastership, is found in this very ability to dispense Masonic light and knowledge correctly, gracefully and abundantly.

YEARNINGS.

Brothers, when o'er my head
The silent dust is spread,
And this poor heart its quiverings shall forbear,
Where'er my body lie,
Though far the Grave away,
I would, dear Brothers, be remembered *here!*

Brothers, when tender sighs
Around me shall arise,
And speak of what I did, or fain would do,
Such honest, truthful words,
As Masons' tongue affords,
I would, dear Brothers, have rehearsed by *you!*

CHAPTER VI.

ATTENDING GRAND LODGE.

A Mason's relation to his Grand Lodge is a thing but little understood. Its importance is largely overestimated in some quarters; in others it is as largely underestimated. By some the Grand Lodge is viewed as a power of boundless extent, and its deliverances, often adopted by insignificant majorities and for unworthy ends, as so many oracles. By others it is viewed as only an annual representative conclave met to arrange the financial affairs of the Craft and settle cases of discipline appealed to it. Neither of these extremes of opinion is right: the truth lies between.

A concise definition of Grand Lodge powers is thus given: " It is supreme within its Constitution." That is, it may visit with penalties of Expulsion all derelictions from the rules established within its Constitution, and other Grand Lodges the world over will justify and sustain it in so doing, *provided nothing is assumed in its Constitution beyond the ancient Landmarks.** This definition forbids any Grand Lodge legislation

---

* It is vitally important that this latter distinction be made. All powers assumed in excess of this are not merely surplusage, they are despotism. In our visits to Grand Lodges we have been shocked at the deliberate like assumptions of uncon-

outside of the ancient landmarks and secures to it competent powers to enforce its deliverances within those bounds. Every Mason will love, honor and obey his Grand Lodge whether from fear or love ; from *love* because the Grand Lodge is his Masonic mother; from *fear* because the Grand Lodge is his Masonic ruler.*

The Model Master during his whole term will keep his mind upon the duty of preparing for Grand Lodge. He will see that the Secretary properly transcribes all papers and reports designed for that body. If cases have been appealed, he will look over the transcripts and correct them where needed. The Annual Report with its footings-up will have his inspection, and the proper dues to Grand Lodge will be taken by him from the Treasurer and borne to the Grand Secretary. Having seen to it in due season that the last annual Proceedings of Grand Lodge have been read and explained to the Lodge, he will see that votes be properly taken and recorded upon such propositions, if any, as may have been submitted to

---

stitutional powers, claimed by Masons whose general learning and experience should have warned them from the rock upon which so many wrecks have been made. In general we may say that for every unconstitutional claim made by a Grand Lodge it forfeits a corresponding portion of the love, fear and respect of its constituents.

* If in our free comments upon Grand Lodge errors we seem to be deficient in respect for that body, we beg leave to deprecate such a judgment. None respects more highly or will make more sacrifices of everything but landmarks to sustain it. One may love the *person* and yet dislike the *failings* of another.

the subordinate Lodges. If important questions of Masonic law or duty are to be settled by Grand Lodge, he will be sure to gather the wishes of his Lodge in relation to them, that he may render his vote accordingly. Without this assurance he cannot be said to *represent* his Lodge at all. Too often the Grand Lodge is made up of members who represent nothing but their own views, and these shaped by the craft of a few master-minds experienced in wire-working and log-rolling.*

The Model Master will of course make himself thoroughly familiar with the Constitution of his Grand Lodge. Without it he is afloat on the sea of events without sail or helm. The best Masters of our acquaintance have committed the principal portions of that important document to memory; such can never be taken by surprise to be made to vote in the dark. To study this subject well, read the thirty-nine Articles compiled first by George Payne, A. D. 1720, and approved by the

---

* If not, whence this continual change in Grand Lodge legislation? Why does this session vote down the proceedings of the last? There is nothing in meteorology more fluctuating and uncertain than Grand Lodge legislation! Does any one think this would be so were delegates truly to *represent* their Lodges? If Masters would take pains to learn the sentiments of the brethren upon propositions this evil might be remedied.

The G. L. of England (likewise Canada,) has a custom that might well be initiated here: Every question that is to come before Grand Lodge is noted down upon an *Agenda paper* and made known to the Lodge several months before Grand Lodge assembles. Thus no question can be suddenly sprung upon the brethren there, as with us,—and the overpowering influence of the few practiced members is comparatively nullified.

Grand Lodge of England, Dec. 27, 1721. Out of these 39 Articles more than 25 are directed to the government, powers and duties of the Grand Lodge and its officers.* Three of these conclusions are most important :

1. All the tools used in Working shall be approved by the Grand Lodge.†

2. Appeals from the decisions of Lodges are to the Grand Lodge.

3. The Grand Lodge cannot change the ancient landmarks.

The ancient title given to the Grand Lodge (*Assemblie*) is suggestive of all that social joy, unrestrained communication, leveling of varied ranks and harmony of diverse interests that make up the inestimable advantages of Grand Lodge meetings. We have rarely failed to find in Grand Lodges an air of cheerfulness pervading the sittings. If no other advantages accrued to Masonry from these annual meetings than that of making Masons better acquainted with each other it would justify even greater trouble and expense. Friendships are there established more lasting than time. Hearts are cemented

---

* A glance at the ordinary legislation of Grand Lodges will show that very many of their deliverances are in direct violation not only of the ancient landmarks but of their own Constitutions.

† This implies that the moral and spiritual doctrines taught ·in the Lodge can not be exceeded or diminished beyond the standard set by the Grand Lodge ; that Grand Lodge, as in the 3d Rule, being itself restricted to the standard of the ancient landmarks.

together that would otherwise revolve in a remote relationship. Other advantages result; jarring ideas are reconciled; comets reduced to planets; crude and imperfect theories corrected; innovations frowned down; errors adjusted; appeals heard and adjudicated; light on Masonry disseminated; and best of all, peace and harmony are made to prevail throughout the bounds of the entire jurisdiction.

As far back as the XIVth century these results of Grand Lodge assemblages were anticipated and the following Ordinance established: " Once a year ye are to assemble together to consult how ye may best work to serve the Craft and to your own profit and credit." It gives no shallow insight into the ancient purity of Masonic labor to know that the same authority which ordained the above rule also declared: " Ye shall be true to and love each other. Ye shall call each other *Brother* or *Fellow*, not *Slave* or any unkind name....Ye shall truly deserve your reward of the Master ye serve....Each Brother shall treat the peculiarities of the other with the gentleness, decency and forbearance he claims for his own.... Ye shall have reasonable pay and live honestly." Happy in any age the Masonic constituency that has a Grand Lodge to ordain and enforce such precepts!

The amenities of Grand Lodge gatherings are well expressed in the following passage: " The company of Masons, being otherwise termed *Free* masons, of ancient standing and good reckoning by means of affable and kind meetings, divers times and as a loving brotherhood use to do, did frequent this mutual Assembly (the Grand Lodge) in the time of Henry VI., in the XIIth year of his reign, (A. D. 1434.)"

If we have been successful in the present article we have given our readers a foretaste of peculiar pleasure to be enjoyed at Grand Lodge. Shall we now point out how you may be useful and honored? You will find, as a general rule, a few old members of Grand Lodge claiming on the score of long experience a large share of the government, attention and honors. Now, the business of a Grand Lodge is in itself so simple, so easy, so clearly defined by its own Constitution, that this is not a necessary consequence in a Grand Lodge. *Every member should claim his share in what is going on, for one member shoulders as much responsibility as another.* No question should be allowed more than its proper attention because offered by an influential man, and no question should have less than its merited attention because offered by a new-comer, or a non-influential man. With such a rule as this in view, every delegate will be able to keep his mind upon a due balance, and the system of cliques, too common in Grand Lodges, will be broken up in his. The solemn reservation that you made in your Installation Covenant, viz. : " You admit that it is not in the power of any man *or body of men* to make innovations in the body of Masonry," will be your justification for any protest against unconstitutional legislation.

One of the first things that will strike your attention at Grand Lodge is the singular and often comical attachment of its old members to what we shall call, for want of a better name "local landmarks," or peculiar observances. Every Grand Lodge has them. How they originated nobody knows; but as no two Grand Lodges have the same, it is easy to see that they are spurious. We shall not describe them here,—indeed many of them are esoteric—but will say in general terms that whatever a Grand Lodge has which is different from all others, is *local and not authoritative*. While a decent respect for your Masonic mother requires you to observe and conform to them while there, yet you will do your Lodge at home much mischief if you transplant them.

In selecting officers for the Grand Lodge you will of course be influenced by the ancient and established rule, and vote for no one "for seniority, but only for merit." No other rule is safe.

We close this article by quoting XV. Rules, by which a Master and consequently a Grand Master may be tested:

RULE 1.—*The Master must be a moral and a good man.*—He is an exemplar to his flock. "Like master like man" is a rule older than Æsop, wiser than Plato. If in his daily walks and conversation he fails to practice *out of* the Lodge what he teaches *in* it, his labor is vain, his seat is practically empty; his Lodge is a body without a head.

How absurd as a practical idea that of electing an immoral man, a blasphemer, drunkard, licentious man, etc., to the east!

Nothing is so destructive to the growth in numbers, the increase in finances, the standing in point of honor, or the social enjoyments of the Craft at labor or refreshment as the influence of an immoral head. The stream can not rise higher than the fountain.

A Lodge never will be better than its Master, who is viewed by the community as the embodiment of the Order when visible on public occasions.

RULE 2.—*The Master must be a law-abiding man.*—In all the riots and mobs, in all the exhibitions of Lynch law, in all the violations of statute and common law with which our country at times is afflicted, the Master of a Lodge should be found on the conservative side. He must never be chargeable with an infraction of the citizen's duty, but cheerfully conform to the laws of the country in which he resides and dilligently teach others so. With what propriety else can he say to his Initiates that "Masonry interferes with no duty a man owes to his country."

RULE. 3.—*The Master of a Lodge must be no Conspirator.*— Midnight treasons, secret plots, schemes of self-aggrandizement at the expense of one's country—all these are abhorrent to the sense of him who appreciates that he is solemnly pledged to the responsible duty of the Masonic East. It is his part to prove to a vigilant government that the secrecy of Masonry is not the secrecy of an assassin ; that its bonds are not bonds of piracy ; that its wages are not the thirty pieces of silver of a Judas.

RULE 4.—*The Master of a Lodge must be of good report before all men.*—In the nervous language of our Monitors, " he must work diligently, live creditably, and act honorably by all men." It is this that will recommend our Fraternity to the hearts of a moral world; it is this that will afford him the means of disseminating that charity to the distressed so often demanded, so acceptable to the Most High, so self-rewarding to the philanthropic giver. But if the Master be idle or extravagant he holds up the body of which he is the acknowledged head as a fit object of contempt.

RULE 5.—*The Master must be meek and temperate.*—" Meek as Moses, temperate as the sons of Rechab," are prime recommendations of him who sits on Solomon's seat. His gavel is supposed to have knocked all the rough corners from its builder's mind and conscience, and brought him the golden rewards of self-discipline. Therefore his brethren will honor him.

RULE 6.—*The Master of the Lodge must be cautious, courteous and faithful and must practice self-government.*—In his behavior *cautious;* lest the vigilant eye mark the weak spot, the flawy place, and disgrace follow his relations to his Masonic Brethren. *Courteous;* for have they not chosen him, honored him, promised to obey him, and thus earned his grateful politeness and fraternal love in his relations to the Lodge? *Faithful,* for he is pledged before God so to be; he is esoterically and exoterically bound by every tie that can shackle an honest man so to be. All the precepts of the Sinaitic law are so many injunctions to self-government which he must consider as directed to himself; every speculative application of an operative implement he must make to his own mind, and so skillful must he be in this shadowy use of Masonic tools as that nothing but death can divest him of his title: *a Master in Israel.*

RULE. 7.—*The Master of the Lodge must possess an ardent love for genuine Masonry.*—To this end he must learn to abhor all imposters, and discountenance all innovations. Being able by affection, study and experience to distinguish the pure gold from the base, he must have a genuine admiration for the pure and honest, and contempt for the base in Masonry. It is a bad sign to see the Master of the Lodge seeking with a prurient curiosity, the shallow pools of imitative associations. Rather should his heart, soul and mind be seen engrossed in the work to which he has pledged his best energies, that of Free-Masonry.

RULE 8.—*The Master of the Lodge must respect his superiors in Masonry.*—How shall he be obeyed who has not himself learned the duty of obedience. Out of the three sources of authority upon which the Master predicates his right to govern, two are *from above* viz.: The Grand Lodge through its charter, the Deity through His Word. Thus while he commands once he obeys twice.

RULE 9.—*The Master of the Lodge must be a zealot.*—It is his part to propagate the knowledge of Masonry far and wide.

He is the apostle of this Gospel; close in debate, exact in logic; well read in exoteric knowledge; familiar with mankind; who so fit as he to battle against opposition and overcome it.

3

None of your cold blooded indifference in the east of a M.
sonic Lodge.

RULE 10.—*The Master of the Lodge must be versed in t*
Landmarks of Masonry.—He must often "walk around Jer
salem" and mark the bulwarks thereof! he must know h
ground well, how far the pillars are from the center—and
one be removed by accident or design, raise the warning voic
without delay, that it be restored.

RULE 11.—*The Master of the Lodge must be a lover of ol*
time things.—Progressiveness, in the modern sense of th
term, has no meaning in Masonry.

The religion of Abraham was "to learn the will of God :
to perform it followed in his mind in due course. The Masonr
of a true craftsman is *to know the Landmarks.*

He will assuredly love them and obey them.

RULE 12.—*The Master of the Lodge must be zealous of i*
honor.—He will cherish its chastity as a thing, like a virgin's
above reproach.

Visitors and applicants for membership will be received wit
zealous scrutiny, and only when perfectly known, will they b
permitted to enjoy the honors and rewards accumulated wit
so much toil and care in the Masonic Lodge.

RULE. 13.—*The Master of the Lodge must communica*
statedly with the Grand Lodge.—He must be one who has th
ability and the mind to attend the sessions of that body be
far or near.

RULE 14.—*The Master of the Lodge will brook no clandestin*

neighbors.—Feeling the importance of Masonic purity, he has no heart or hand for the Samaritans, whose tribe and kindred are polluted, or whose genealogy can not be traced up.

RULE 15.—*The Master of the Lodge will maintain the regularity of the Masonic system as an essential portion of itself.*—" A place for everything and everthing in its place," "nothing in Masonry without a rational explanation," are as lamps to his feet.

———————

A PARTING HYMN.

Refreshed with angels' food we go,
To serve Thee in thy work below ;
Trusting, when Sabbath-rest is given,
To share Thy richer joys in Heaven.

Then, bind our willing souls in one ;
Confirm the COVENANTS here begun ;
Each day those vows more sacred be,
Cemented in eternity.

CHAPTER VII.

PUBLIC DEMONSTRATIONS,

The ability to display the Masonic Brethren properly before the world is a very different and far more difficult thing than the ability to go creditably through the "Master's part" in a public exhibition. The latter can be done and is done by very many Masters who do not aspire to the name of "Model ," the former is worthy the study of a "Model Master," even the best. It is a rare thing in the world; so rare that we have never seen it more than a short half dozen times in our life. The present Chapter will be devoted to this theme.

There are only five occasions on which Masons, as such, should come out in public. They are these:

First.—In the burial of a deceased Mason who died in affiliation with his Lodge, and died an honorable death.

Second.—In planting the Corner Stone of a Masonic edifice, or some public edifice or structure, such as a Town Hall, Canal Lock, Monument, Bridge, or Harbor structure, Rail Road building, etc., etc.

Third.—In dedicating a Masonic Hall.

Fourth.—In consecrating a new Lodge and installing its officers. Likewise in installing the officers of any Lodge.

Fifth.—In celebrating the St. John's Days by Procession, Address and Feast.

We will comment upon each of these in the order given. We place the Funeral Service first, on account of its frequency in practice, although the *Monitor*, for good reasons, sets it last. The Model Master will not wait until the shaft of death reaches one of his Brethren before he studies the Funeral service. One of the best of the class who has honored the East of his Lodge, and the Grand East of his jurisdiction, began on the day of his election to commit to memory the Funeral "Invocations" and "Responses." The most intelligent Masters we ever heard, make it a matter of duty to commit the whole "Service" to memory, so that no book or aid will be needed in public. This we always recommend. You will not make a good display of yourself or the craft before the world, if you have to read aloud from the *Monitor*.

When the message comes " A Column is broken : a Brother is dead !" the Model Master will make it a point to get if possible every member of his Lodge to attend the Funeral ; likewise as many from neighboring Lodges as practicable. Less than fifty Masons do not make a good public display, though we often have to put up with half the number. Demitted Masons are not wanted on these occasions (or in fact any other) and you will not invite them, though if they come they can not well be thrust aside. If possible, fill all the *pro tem.* offices for the occasion with members of your own Lodge.

See that your Lodge is open and ready for duty at the hour

previously appointed by the family of the deceased. It is a public scandal, frequent enough, that on such occasions the Lodge is shamefully tardy.

Allow no other Society to precede you or to take the Burial Service out of your hands. Refuse to attend the Funeral at all, as Masons, unless the Masonic Fraternity is allowed its ancient prerogative. It is consummate impudence in modern Societies whose only merits are borrowed from Masonry, to assume the Burial of our dead with their manufactured Rites.

Select your very best man for Marshal. Nay, if you cannot get a " very best" man for that office give the gavel to your Senior Warden and take the baton (that is, act as Marshal) yourself. More depends on the skill, activity and fidelity of that officer in making public demonstrations effective than upon all the other officers united.* Instruct your Lodge care-

---

* See the directions in the *Miniature Monitor*, pp. 124 *et seq.* under this head. They are full and explicit. The prefatory remarks in that work concerning *Funerals*, are here quoted: "The solemn and impressive rite of Burial is admittedly the most instructive ceremony known to Masonry. It is so arranged in its symbolisms as to convey the great doctrines of Masonry—morality, benevolence, sympathy, brotherly love, the immortality of the soul and the resurrection of the body. It teaches the power of Love to overreach the tomb, and to write upon the tablets of the human heart all the good deeds of a departed Brother. In practice, the Funeral Service of Masons is not usually well given. It is rarely the case, that suitable attention is paid to its details ; and oftener the unskilful manner in which the Ceremonial is performed wounds and disappoints beholders."

ully before they go out in public to observe the strictest deco-
um, to avoid all conversation, to march in orderly manner,
nd to give the strictest attention to the orders of the Marshal.
)f course, such indecencies as smoking, laughter, leaving the
anks, and the like, if you have any members mean enough to
:ommit them, must be sternly forbidden.

Bear in mind, that if you act as Master on the occasion,
our place is necessarily and at all times, until you reach the
;rave, *in the rear*. Therefore, whatever irregularities may oc-
:ur, you are helpless to correct them, *save through the Marshal.*
(ou are, in fact, so situated as to be incapable of knowing a
ithe of the improprieties that occur until it is too late to cor-
ect them. Our own mortification and anguish at being obliged,
n a certain occasion, to walk a mile through a great city in
he rear of a procession, without the ability to correct a thous-
nd irregularities in plain view of us, because the Marshal
)ersisted in marching *before the Tyler*, gives us a keen ap-
)reciation of what Masters must suffer who, are afflicted
vith ignorant or intractable Marshals. The proper instruc-
ions to your Marshal are "keep in motion from the head of
he column to the foot, and communicate personally with me
t least as often as every ten minutes." This constant motion
)y the Marshal, enables him to see and correct irregularities
ıs they occur: these frequent conferences with the Master in-
orm him of his duty relative thereto. In general, the pro-
:ession will fall into good array, and begin to make a creditable
lisplay by the time they have marched a quarter of a mile,

that is, if you have a good Marshal to direct them. Take care that the pace is not too swift, a frequent fault.

At the grave, let your addresses, prayers, invocations, etc., be grave and dignified. The Public Grand Honors *must* be done slowly or they will appear ridiculous. On the return home allow no straying from the ranks, and give no Brother leave to withdraw without the best of reasons by him rendered.

Do not allow your Lodge to use any Burial Service save that in Webb's Monitor unless, indeed, your Grand Lodge requires it, which does not occur in many jurisdictions. Cross, in his *Chart*, has done mischief, followed by other publishers in the same line, in making changes and innovations here. All that matter of throwing an Apron into the grave is to be discarded. There is a simplicity and fitness in Webb's Service vainly sought elsewhere. Use that and nothing else, oh, Model Master!

In the ceremony of planting a Corner Stone* the same general principles are applicable. To secure an efficient Marshal is always the first requisite. Other things being equal, military men make the best. Give your Marshal as many assistants as he may desire. If the procession includes civic parades, military, etc., each department must have its own Marshal and Assistants, all to be subject to a Chief Marshal, who should be, a Mason. In all mixed processions the Masonic de-

---

* The term " Planting" is growing into popular favor. It is elegantly appropriate.

partment *must come last in line.* If this post of honor is denied you, we advise you to refuse to permit your Lodge to join in the ceremonial. The dignity and honor of the Craft demand this of you, and no Model Master will prove recreant. We were once, to our disgrace, compelled to walk in a Corner Stone procession in which the Masonic portion was placed, we think intentionally, perhaps only ignorantly, inferior to the youngest of all the imitative Societies present ; and this too, when the proposed Monument was that of a distinguished Mason, a Past Grand Master! Never again will we submit to such a disgrace.†

The ceremonies of Dedication, Consecration and Installation require no further advice than that already given. In all cases where the Craft is to come publicly forth, it will be well to recollect that if you make an effective display of your Lodge you will be likely to increase your numbers by the increment of many good and desirable men of the community. It is the very life and growth of a Lodge to show itself properly before the world.

In preparing for the ceremony of Festivals the Model Master will see that suitable toasts are prepared, and when practicable, experienced Brethren designated to respond to them. The Lodge should be especially notified that they do not go to the

---

† Our rule has ever been to submit silently to the orders of the day. But this has led us into errors which have been copied to our own confusion by those of our friends who suppose we always do *what we think is right.* We do what we are ordered, and show up errors afterwards.

table for eating and drinking only, but to share that mental refreshment, those social joys that make up the burden of the old Masonic songs, and that formed so large a part of the pleasures of Masonry in days gone by. Designate persons to sing. Call forth volunteer sentiments. Seek for original Odes and thoughts in any form. Make your Banquet a thing to be remembered for something else than the indigestion and stomach-pains that follow the "eat-and-run-away" dinners, of which we have so often partaken. Several hours can be profitably spent at a Masonic Banquet when properly conducted.

We wholly disapprove of mixed parties at Masonic Banquets. The presence of wife, daughter, sister, and sweetheart, however agreeable elsewhere, is *not* an addition to the pleasure of these occasions. Things ought to be said, things will be said at such times that have reference to the secrets of Masonry. A word to the wise is sufficient. Our Canadian Brethren understand these matters better than we Americans do, and they take care to *tyle* their Masonic Banquets and give themselves ample time to enjoy them.

We conclude the present Chapter with the general remark, that whatever is worth doing at all, is worth doing well. If it is thought proper for you to lead your Lodge forth in public to meet the scrutiny of eyes, friendly and unfriendly, it is more than proper that you should do it in a manner to reflect credit and not discredit upon them and the Society at large. A Funeral well conducted, has been known to bring twelve good applicants knocking at the door of the Lodge. A Corner-

stone duly planted, has changed the sentiment of an entire unmasonic neighborhood. A Banquet well managed, has cemented together, in happy and useful bonds, a disjointed and
unfruitful Lodge membership.

———•●●———

A city set upon a hill
    Cannot be hid ;
Exposed to every eye, it will
Over surrounding plain and vale,
    An influence shed ;
And spread the light of peace afar,
Or blight the land with horrid war.

Each Masons' Lodge is planted so
    For high display ;
Each is a beacon light, to show
Life's weary wanderers, as they go,
    The better way ;
To show, by ties of earthly love,
How perfect is the LODGE above.

Be this your willing task, dear friends,
    While laboring here ,
Borrow from Him who kindly lends
The heavenly Ladder that ascends
    The higher sphere ;
And let the world your progress see,
UPWARD, by Faith, Hope, Charity.

CHAPTER VIII.

THE FURNITURE OF A LODGE.

There is a portion of the third section of the Entered Apprentice's Lecture which runs in this wise : "The furniture of a Lodge is the Holy Bible, Square and Compass."* Judging from the meagerness of the furnishing of some Lodges we have visited, it would appear that some Brethren think the above is *all* the furniture a Lodge needs. So shabby, so contemptible is the appearance of many Masonic halls that we are sure the foot of woman never treads them ; that no eye ever views them by daylight; that no disposing, directing hand of Steward is ever busy about them. For nearly three hundred days of the year the mice and insects have their own way. Will the reader pardon us for quoting a description of one of these " foul nests" taken from our own memorandum book of " things we have witnessed."

"The appearance of the Hall of —— Lodge, No. ——,

---

* We caution our readers against the wretched innovation of styling the Compass *Compasses.* As well call scissors *scissorses!* Bible language and Masonic language alike agree in the word *Compass.* Read *Isaiah xliv*, 13 : " The carpenter stretcheth out his *rule ;* he marketh it out with the *line ;* he fitteth it with *planes,* and he marketh it out with the *compass.*"

merits the severest condemnation. It is exactly what every Lodge room is that is never swept or garnished. From the lowermost step of the stairs, which ascend outside the house, under a sort of shed roof, to the uppermost step of the three that ascend the Dais, dirt of every variety of cohesion and color abounds. All the farming lands in the county appear to be represented in these deposits of mother earth. The Bible is foul with pollution. The aprons trailing here and there on the floor can in no wise be made "to protect the garments of the workmen;" they would rather *soil* them with their contact. There is no G over the East, no Sheaf over the South, no Columns in the West and South. The Lodge possesses no Rods for its Deacons, nor Pillars, nor Carpet for instruction. Its jewels are of tin. Its sword is of the period of the Revolutionary War. A sliding pannel in the door enables the lethargic Tyler to perform his traditional duties with little trouble to the Junior Deacon or to himself. The Secretary has a rickety, cramped-up table in the South-east, apparently a defunct wash-stand, but without the drawers; the Treasurer has not even so much as that.

The Altar (?) is a nail keg covered, not ingeniously, with red cloth to conceal (but it does *not* conceal) the staves; it totters if only the weight of a hand is laid upon the dirty Bible that surmounts it. The Lights (?) are tallow-candles (mutton tallow of all the tallows) small, badly-wicked, whose rancid fumes sicken and poison the confined atmosphere. There are no printed By-Laws; there is no copy of the Constitution; there are no Working Tools; there are no copies of Grand Lodge Proceedings in the Hall. The seats against the wall are but rough benches, scanty in number, uneasy in position. The Gavels are apparently made of knobs taken from the branches of old oak trees, and fastened to the ends of drum sticks; they fly off with dangerous facility whenever any use is made of them. There is no Charter visible in the room!*

In visiting a new Lodge (we have visited so many), our eye, from long experience, has become trained to detect beauties or faults at a glance. Shall we tell our readers (so far as such things may lawfully be told in writing,) how we do it!†

In the ante-room we observe whether the Tyler is comfortable in his seat—is his room warm? has he the traditionary instrument of his office? does he keep it in his hand? Are the Aprons laid orderly upon a table? are the coats, hats, &c., neatly hung about the apartment? If there is anything wanting to the Tyler in all this, then the furnishing of the Lodge is

---

* Need we apologize for using such plain language in pointing out the faults of the Brethren! Our motive is not to shame the Brethren, but to shame them into improvement. What can an intelligent candidate think of a set of men who at home are neat and proper in their appearance, but whose Lodge is less neat than their stables! If "cleanliness is next to godliness," as the modern Paul expresses it, that virtue deserves at least an indorsement by Masons.

† It is the most provoking thing to the Masonic writer that the very counsels most needed by the Craft relate to the esoterical subjects of Masonry. No man can *write* upon these themes so well as the poorest *lecturer* can teach.

by that much deficient. Entered into the hall, the eye catches at one sweep the Pillars, the Columns, the G, the Sheaf, the Carpet on the Wall, the Altar, the three Stations and the Dais. Anything defective here shows itself in the first glance. Arrived at the Altar, its furnishing comes under a critical notice as we look down upon it.

Arrived at the East and seated, the *tout ensemble* fills the eye, and every defect is there apparent. Almost every Lodge is defective in something; many are defective in the majority of objects that are absolutely needed for Masonic instruction. We will not, however, too minutely specify them.

Now, all these defects which are evident to the experienced eye in the few minutes devoted to this examination are to be remedied by the zeal, wisdom and power of the "Model Master." No one else so well knows, no one else so much cares for the matter as he does. If he possesses the "pride of excellence," he will not suffer a year to pass away until all needful things are supplied him.

The most expensive objects are a pair of large and well pro portioned Pillars to be set near the north-west door of entrance. If purchased of dealers they cost too much for ordinary Lodges to bear. But they can be made at home. Any man who can turn a bed post can turn the shafts. Any carpenter who can make the moulding of a chimney piece can make the base and entablature. Then a pair of cheap school globes and a dollar's worth of white paint, and you are as well fitted, symbolically, as though the "Widow's Son" had been your architect.

To carpet the floor, many substitutes can be found for expensive ingrains. Cotton bagging serves well enough for country Lodges, and even tanbark evenly distiibuted over the floor is better than nothing. No visitor will feel like ridiculing the Lodge which resorts to such shifts in the absence of the ability to do better. The most ridiculous object to our minds is a Lodge room immensely large, uncarpeted and unfurnished, looking like an empty snail shell on a dry patch of sand.*

Among the objects of furniture not to be neglected is the Library. Every Lodge *must* have a Library, if it contains nothing more than a Monitor, the Constitution of the Grand Lodge, the By-laws of your own Lodge and the Proceedings of the Grand Lodge since its organization. These, we say, *must* be in possession of every Lodge, else the work cannot properly go on. But to these should be added many and many a precious object dispensing Masonic light. The literature of the Masonic Institution in modern times is rich in publications upon the history, philanthropy, jurisprudence and *belles lettres* of Freemasonry. The *Universal Masonic Library* has fifty-three of such works within its broad lids, sold too at prices that every Lodge can afford to pay.

---

* We have already remarked in this series of papers upon the mania, which the Civil war has happily checked, of building Masonic Halls. We look upon the Lodge which lays the foundation stone of a Hall (to be built at its own expense), as beginning its own destruction. The expense will be a millstone about its neck. There are but few Lodges which are exceptions to this rule.

Another object, next to a Library in importance, is a Melodeon. The whole subject of *Music in its relation to Masonry*, deserves more attention than we have time to give it here. Its charming influences are not half appreciated by those who have control of Masonic matters in the various jurisdictions. The passages relative to music in the Fellow Crafts' Lecture sound strangely to us, when we reflect that the science has gone into almost total disuse among the Craft. In older times it was not so. Masons sung at their Work; sung at their Refreshments; sung at their Festivals; sung at their Funerals. Music then filled the place which the great author of our being doubtless intended for it, and served as a medium for conveying to the heart the most enobling sentiments. A Melodeon in the Lodge, played with even a modicum of skill, is a well spring of pleasure from which the Brethren will draw on every occasion that justifies it.*

And while recommending certain objects as essential to the correct furnishing of a Lodge we would deprecate the practice which prevails in some quarters, of lumbering the room with unmeaning and superflous furniture. Everything should have symbolical reference to something in Masonry. Everything on the walls, ceiling or floor, should be such as the Master can refer to in the course of his instructions, to give point to them,

---

* It will not be out of place here to refer to the "Harmonium," a late improvement upon the Melodeon, which is most happily adapted, and at a very low price, to the wants of the Lodge room.

and enforce them. Anything outside of these, is not only superflous, but produces confusion.

A closing remark under this head. In soliciting contributions to furnish a Lodge, almost every person will give some· thing *in kind*, while but few care to give *money*. Almost every one will give a book, a chair, a picture, or a lot of plank, carpeting, etc. Many will give a day's work who will give nothing else. These benevolences, properly used, will go far to the fitting up, and adorning and furnishing your Lodge.

EARNESTNESS OF COVENANTING.

Never will I break the Covenant,
    Plighted, Brother, with thee now!
ONE between us stands, attesting
    To the fervor of my vow:
In his name, *above* his Promise,
    By his honor, *for* his cause,
Here's my hand, the Lord confirm it,—
    I will surely keep my vows!

CHAPTER IX.

VITALIZING THE LODGE.

In the first eight chapters of these series we have spoken of the true method of *setting up the machinery*, so to speak, of a Masonic Lodge. We have enlarged upon the importance of paraphernalia and equipments; of correct instructions in Open ing and Closing your Meetings; of Funerals and other public demonstrations; of dignity and tact in the Master; of attendance upon the Grand Lodge, and other themes essential to the perpetuity of the Institution. The *machine* being thus set up and perfected, all its wheels and cranks and pulleys, etc., in place, it remains now to show how to *run it*. A mere machine is a dead thing; its usefulness and value are estimated by its *works*.

We have seen more than one Lodge, of which no flaw or defect could be predicated, except that *it was doing no good in the world*. Its paraphernalia was costly and made *secundem artem*. Its Lectures and instructions, its demonstrations, public and private, were sufficiently formal and precise; its outward semblance was that of a statue of elegant symmetry and proportion, but *it had no vitality*. For all practical purposes it was *nothing*. Our present chapter is devoted to the subject of *breathing life into a Lodge ;* of setting Lodge-machinery in motion ; giving a useful aim to the laborious and expensive structure of which you have been made the engineer.

Did you ever ask yourself, oh Master of Masons, for what purposes your Lodge was established and has been thus far maintained ? If not, let us inquire together. For unless we can answer that question, we shall make no headway in comprehending the theme to which the present chapter is devoted.

A close examination of the Ancient Charges, Constitutions, and historical evidences of Masonry will give us this for a reply : "Masonry is a system, teaching symbolically, Piety, Morality, Science, Charity and Self-discipline."* A few quotations in proof of this will be proper here :

"A Mason is obliged by his tenure (that is by the very terms of his reception and continuance) to obey the Moral Law.... Masons are obliged to that religion in which all men agree ....Masons must be good men and true, or men of honor and honesty....Masonry is a centre of union and the means of conciliating true friendship among persons that must have remained at a perpetual distance. The craftsmen by their peaceableness and loyalty have practically answered the cavils of their adversaries and promoted the honor of the fraternity who ever flourished in times of peace....The persons admitted

---

* See *Code of Masonic Law* under Landmark Second, in which this subject is pursued at much length. That whole Division of the *Code* refers to this.

members of a Lodge must be good and true men. . . .All pre-
ferment among Masons is grounded upon real worth and personal merit only. . . .A Master or Warden is chosen for his
merit. . . .All Masons shall work honestly on working days. . . .
The Craftsmen are to avoid all ill language and to call each
other by no disobliging names but *brother* or *fellow.* . . .None
shall discover envy at the prosperity of a brother, nor supplant
him, nor put him out of his work, if he be capable to finish the
same. . . .You are not to behave yourselves ludicrously or
jestingly while the Lodge is engaged in what is serious and
solemn. . . .No private piques or quarrels must be brought
within the door of the Lodge, far less any quarrels about
religion, or nations, or state policy. . . .At home you are to act
as becomes a moral and wise man. . . .You are to cultivate
brotherly love, the foundation and capestone, the cement and
glory of this ancient fraternity, avoiding all wrangling and
quarreling, all slander and backbiting, not permitting others
to slander any honest brother, but defending his character and
doing him all good offices as far as is consistent with your
honesty and safety, and no farther. . . .You must say and do
nothing which may hinder brotherly love and good offices from
being renewed and continued. . . .Patiently listen to the honest and friendly advice of Master and Fellows when they would
prevent your going to law with strangers, or would excite
you to put a speedy period to all law suits."

From these texts, and others like them that might be quoted at great length, are deduced the thousands of Masonic

addresses, lectures and essays which treat of the *morality* and *religion* of the order. Upon the *truth* of these eloquent and divine doctrines, the permanency of Masonic friendships and the very life of the Masonic institution are based. No covenant of wicked men is enduring ; nor can good men bind themselves by a covenant whose basis is other than piety and morality. *

Now this is the test question applicable to every Lodge : Is your Lodge accomplishing those ends ? Is Piety advanced by the operations of the Lodge ? is Morality ? is Science ? is Charity ? is Self discipline ? If not, then your Lodge is a failure.

No one can say that the Rituals of Masonry do not give ample instructions under these heads. *Piety* (reverence to God and obedience to his Word) is taught both by word and act in very many passages, esoteric and exoteric. *Morality*—why the Ritual is full of it ; the Entered Apprentices Degree is one eloquent lecture upon it. *Science*—the Fellow Craft's Degree is one eloquent Lecture upon it. *Charity*—how could symbology express anything more clearly than the emblems of Masonry express Charity ! *Self-discipline*—the very purpose and aim of Masonry is to discipline (that is *prepare*) its recipients by labor and prayer for "the House not made with hands." As, then, these five great lessons—Piety, Morality, Science, Charity and Self-discipline—are so frequently and forcibly

---

* This is a sufficient reply to the flood of cavilings and detractions of the anti-masonic era.

taught in the Masonic Rituals, we may then call it the test-question, Is your Lodge accomplishing these ends? To *vitalize a Lodge* is to put it in the way of doing so.

No writer can lay down general rules for this. We can only specify such as are likely to apply to the majority of cases. A few rules are inserted here which will guide the reader in *vitalizing his Lodge :*

1. ENCOURAGE VISITATIONS.

The *Ancient Constitutions,* * Article XI, say : "All particu-lar Lodges are to observe the same usages....in order to which, and for cultivating a good understanding among Free-masons, some members out of every Lodge shall be deputed to visit the other Lodges as often as shall be thought convenient.'

Treat visitors with marked courtesy and attention ; they will help to vitalize your membership in all the graces of cour-tesy, charity and improvement in Rituals. Invite them to give you their experience. †

2. KEEP A CLOSE ACCOUNT WITH ERRING MEMBERS.

To leave the drunkard, debauchee, blasphemer, slanderer,

---

* The *Ancient Constitutions* differ from the *Ancient Charges* in this respect, that the latter are unchangeable and obliga-tory upon Masons, the former may be enlarged, amended or reduced at the pleasure of the Grand Lodge. The former stand in the relation of Grand Lodge *Constitutions*, which may be and are changed at every meeting.

† The aged are peculiarly susceptible to the minor courtesies of the Lodge. We recall with tender emotion the pleased look of such an one when alluded to by name in the Lodge or in a public Address.

etc., undisciplined, is to take the very vitality from the Lodge. It is to throw pebbles among the wheels of the machine ; a full stop will occur to all useful movements.

Would that we could convince the Masonic world that *a moral institution can not be conducted by immoral men.*

3. REWARD THE FAITHFUL AND TRUE MEMBERS.

Show them due respect. Defer to their judgment. Give them seats of honor in the Lodge. * When sick, visit them. When dead, bestow those honors, the highest as they are the last which Masonry provides for good Masons.

4. DISPENSE PURE AND ABUNDANT MASONIC LIGHT.

5. ENCOURAGE THE DELIVERY OF MORAL AND SCIENTIFIC LECTURES, PUBLICLY AND IN THE LODGE.

6. INVITE THE CO-OPERATION OF THE FAIR SEX.†

7. PROVIDE ALL NECESSARIES FOR THE COMFORT AND ADORNMENT OF THE LODGE, AND FOR ILLUSTRATING THE LECTURES AND WORK. ‡

8. DISPENSE CHARITIES FREELY. §

---

* Some Masters are so ignorant or negligent as never to ask Past Masters to take seats on the dais.

† We do not particularly refer to the so-called "Adoptive Degrees" or Systems, but to the many methods known to "Model Masters" of securing female influence and co-operation in the charitable deeds of the Craft.

‡ See our last chapter full of remarks under this head.

§ If there are no suffering objects near you, enquire for them in contiguous or distant Lodges. The world has enough destitution and misery to exhaust the beneficence of the most generous.

9. GIVE EVIDENCE BEFORE THE WORLD THAT YOUR PRACTICE CORRESPONDS WITH YOUR PROFESSION.

10. STERNLY REJECT UNWORTHY APPLICANTS.

By these and similar efforts will Masonry in your hands become vitalized. The Lodge will become a delightful place. The members will hasten there early and frequently. Good men from without will knock at your doors. Mothers, sisters and daughters will sing your praises. Usefulness and honor will redound from all your labors and your end will be peace.

Israel then shall dwell in safety alone; the fountain of Jacob shall be upon a land of corn and wine, also his heavens shall drop down dew.

"Happy art thou, oh Israel! who is like unto thee; oh people saved by the LORD the shield of thy help, and who is the sword of thy excellency; and thine enemies shall be found liars unto thee, and thou shalt tread upon their high places. Deut., xxxiii, 28, etc.

TEARS AND SMILES.

The *tear* for friends departed,
The faithful and true-hearted,
Cast midst the rubbish of the silent grave,
Is changed to *smiles* of pleasure,
While trusting that our treasure,
A glorious Resurrection-day will have !

CHAPTER X.

THE TRIAL OF OFFENSES.

It is peculiarly needful in discussing the subject of Trials that we should repeat a caution often given before that " the advice of a Masonic teacher can only be taken where it does not conflict with Grand Lodge regulations." This caution we have ever given in our utterances as editor and lecturer. The advice and warnings of the most eminent writers and speakers have only this extent, no more; they can not be received where they contravene the edicts and deliverances of the Grand Lodge. They are chiefly valuable in those cases which the Grand Lodge has not considered.* For the Master of a Lodge to adopt them and act upon them without first acquainting himself with the statutes of his own Grand Lodge is the most egregious folly, and can lead only to mortifying retractations on his own part, and the want of respect on the part of his brethren.

We repeat this caution here because in the legislation of

---

* They are also useful in shaping the legislation of the Grand Lodge. When a question of amending the Constitution comes up, the quoted opinions of a reliable Masonic jurist often secure the majority of the Grand Lodge without argument. This, indeed, is the chief value of works on Masonic Law.

a few Grand Lodges will be found forms for the Government of Masonic Trials. Such forms, however imperfect or poorly framed, are obligatory upon the Masters of the Lodges under their jurisdiction. To such, the present Chapter can be useful only in a general sense and as affecting those parts of trial not covered by the forms in question.*

With this caution, we proceed with our subject, and first explain *what constitutes an Offense in Masonry.* We specify fourteen classes of Masonic Offenses, viz:

1. Secession from the Order.

2. Disbelief in the Scriptures of God.

3. Blasphemy, Profanity, Irreligious Libertinism.†

4. Theft, Swindling, Dishonesty.

5. Lying, Deceit, Perjury, Falsehood.

6. Adultery, Fornication, Seduction, Licentiousness.

7. Evil Speaking, Scandal, Slander.

8. Covetousness, Uncharitableness.

9. Cruelty, Violence, Bloodshed, Murder.

---

*It is greatly to be desired that Grand Lodges throughout the country should agree upon a uniform system of trials. As it now stands, the subject is in a deplorable condition. What is cause for *suspension* in one State is scarcely cause for *reprimand* in another. The publication of " A Thorough Course of Instruction" upon this subject in 1859, was a step, we believe, in that direction.

†By the term "Irreligious Libertine," an obsolete expression, is understood a person devoid of religious convictions, a skeptic in religious belief, not quite an atheist, but practically a man " without God and without hope in the world."

10. Plots, Conspiracies, Treason.

11. Sabbath Breaking.

12. Indiscretion, Secret-breaking.

13. Contumacy, Disobedience to Lodge and Grand Lodge Orders.

14. Union with Clandestine Associations.

Other classes than these may perhaps be formed, yet we think these sufficiently diffuse. In general, it may be said that " any act is an offense in Masonry which is unjust toward God, one's country or self: any violation of the laws of God, the laws of the nation, or the laws physical, moral and mental, applicable to one's self ; any action contrary to the admitted Word of God, the Statutes and Common Law of the country, or the principles of self-government."

To *prevent offenses* is one chief care of a Master This he labors to do by freqent and earnest exhortations to his members both within and without the Lodge. To *stop the growth of offenses* and confine them within the lower and more excusable classes is the Master's next care. This he strives to do by solemn warnings and appeals to the erring member upon the first evidences of his fault. Thus, if a Brother is known to have been intoxicated, the Master will endeavor to nip the evil in the bud before it runs to the ruinous extent of habitual intemperance. If Brothers have had a verbal altercation, the Master will hasten to offer his mediation and heal the breach before it becomes irreparable.

It is not every offense that should be brought to trial, nor is it every offense that should be brought before the Lodge. In a well-instructed Lodge, where the brethren are taught to counsel each other and to warn each other of approaching danger, there is rarely occasion for a Lodge to proceed to the extremity of a trial. Private warnings and counsel are effectual, as we have personally seen, to check almost every offense as it arises. Blasphemy, Licentiousness, Intemperance, and Violence may be strangled in their birth under the influence of these "fence corner tribunals," in which the exhorter and the exhorted are the only parties (save God), and the gentle spirit of Brotherly Love is the Law.*

But for our present purpose we must suppose an offense really committed, for instance an act of violence, one Brother against another. Let the Junior Warden† bring the charges in some plain form with specifications noting time and place correctly. Almost any form will suffice that is explicit. The following is as good as any:

The undersigned, Junior Warden of —— Lodge, No. ——, at ——, in the performance of his official duties as specified in By-laws, Article —, Section —, solemnly charges Bro. ——, a Master Mason and member of this Lodge,‡ with unmasonic conduct, according to the following specifications:

---

* In England, nearly all questions relative to Masonic discipline are referred to and settled by a Standing Committee.

† For various reasons the Junior Warden is the most appropriate prosecutor.

‡ If a demitted Mason or a Mason of less Degree than the Third, specify the fact.

With striking Bro. ———, a Master Mason and a member of this Lodge, at ———, on the — day of ——, 1866.

And the undersigned, as the official prosecutor of this Lodge, prays that the honor and dignity of the Masonic Institution may be vindicated by the due exercise of Masonic discipline upon the aforesaid Bro. ———.

A——— B———,

(Date.)   *Junior Warden.*

This indictment, for such it is, is handed to the Secretary to be read at a Regular Meeting, and is referred to the Lodge by the Master with the question, What will you do, my Brethren, with these charges against Bro. ———? Some one should move that the charges be received and referred to a committee to examine the evidence. No second to this motion is needed, because the Junior Warden himself is strictly the mover. The Master puts the question to the Lodge. A majority vote controls the question; if favorable, the Master appoints a committee of three to take testimony and report at the next Regular Meeting.* The committee must set the • time and place for taking evidence before leaving the Lodge, and the accused, if present, is notified of time and place that he may be present if he wishes.† Cases sometimes occur where the accused rises at once and admits the offense. If so,

---

* Trials may be had at called meetings if thought best to do so.

† If not present, a certified copy of the charges, &c., must be sent to him.

he should be allowed to state the provocation, if any, and to tender his apology. But his statement, if he makes any, should be inquired into by the committee. If he makes no statement—nothing but a confession—no committee need be appointed, unless some peculiarity in the case should seem to require it. This is a matter for the Lodge to determine.

In all the meetings of the committee the Secretary must be present, as Clerk, to take down the evidence and preserve it for the use of the Lodge.

The committee must have great latitude in the matter of securing evidence ; but if any neglect is apparent on their part, the accused can have it remedied on appeal to the Lodge. Time enough must be given for securing evidence, even though it protracts the case from month to month. The committee, however, should report progress at each Regular Meeting, and then ask further time if necessary.

When prepared to report, a synopsis of their proceedings must be made by the Clerk and subscribed to by each member of the committee, if practicable ; if not, by a majority. This synopsis, together with the testimony, is then read to the Lodge. Upon motion the report is received and the committee discharged. This brings the question fairly before the Lodge for trial.

While the committee is gathering testimony, the accused has the right to cross-examine the witnesses before them. Also to call witnessess of his own to rebut the charges alleged. The accused may have counsel if he chooses, both before the committee and afterwards in the Lodge; but none but Master Masons can act in that capacity.

Upon the discharge of the committee the accused may offer such personal explanations as he pleases, but these are not to be deemed as *evidence*, that is, they are not to be written down and subjected to cross-examination, etc. The accused in such remarks must not impute improper conduct to any Brother, or utter violent or extreme language, under penalty of prejudicing his own case.

This being over, the accused must retire. Then the Master put the question. Is the Brother guilty or not guilty? The answer is given by ballot; a majority vote decides. If the decision is *not guilty*, the record is ordered to be made up, the accused called in and notified of his acquittal. If the decision is *guilty*, a second question is proposed, Shall the Brother be expelled? The answer is made by ballot, the ratio for expulsion being settled by the by-laws. But if the by-laws are silent and the question unsettled by the Grand Lodge having juris- diction, a majority vote decides.* If the decision is *expulsion*, the record is ordered to be made up, and the Secretary, by written communication, notifies the guilty party of the de- cision. But if the decision is *no expulsion*, a third question is proposed, Shall the Brother be suspended? If the majority decide *no suspension*, a fourth question is proposed, Shall the Brother be reprimanded?

---

* We recommend the by-law establishing two-thirds as the proper number for suspension or expulsion.

Should the Lodge decide to *suspend*, the question is then put upon the length of the period of suspension. All these proceedings·should be had deliberately, the counsel of the accused being allowed to remain and scrutinize them. Every member of the Lodge, Master and Junior Warden included, is allowed his vote.*

Such is a skeleton form of trial. It gives the prosecution a fair opportunity to convict the accused of actual offense ; it gives the accused a fair opportunity to palliate his offense if guilty, or to show the weakness and insufficiency of the testi- mony, if innocent. After the verdict of *guilty* is entered and the penalty settled upon, an appeal must be granted, if asked for by the accused or his counsel. The right of appeal can, under no circumstances, be impugned. But the action of the Lodge is binding upon the accused (unless an edict of the Grand Master intervenes) until the Grand Lodge shall reverse it. So, also, an appeal to the Grand Lodge may be taken by the Junior Warden, or any other member of the Lodge, if it is alleged that the Lodge has refused to lay down a penalty for plain guilt.

The Model Master will always advise an accused Brother to plead *guilty* where the case is too palpable for doubt. To

---

* It has been decided in some jurisdictions that because the Junior Warden and the Committee have taken part in the prosecution of the case they are not unprejudiced and ought not to vote ; this ruling is absurd. They vote under the solemnity of their Masonic Covenants.

4

throw one's self upon the good feelings of the Lodge is, in such cases, the most prudent, as it is the most honorable course for a Brother to pursue. A Lodge of Masons, all things considered, is the most gracious and forgiving assemblage of men upon earth. There is no ordinary offense that they will not excuse if a confession and fair show of penitence are made. This we can testify from abundant observation.

In those Lodges, and there are such, in which discipline has long been neglected and the erring permitted to go on for years unchecked, the Master will find great hindrances in setting up a standard of justice. For awhile his Lodge may not second his faithful endeavors to purify the membership. They may pronounce verdicts of *not guilty* where guilt is palpable. Or they may order light and trivial punishments where the offenses are open and gross. In such cases, the Model Master will apply for directions to the Grand Master. He will labor the harder to teach the real purposes of the Masonic Institution. A victory gained in such a Lodge is a victory indeed.

CHAPTER XI.

THE SECRETARY AND TREASURER.

The theory of the Secretary's duties is succinctly given in his response: "To observe the Worshipful Master's will and pleasure; to record the Proceedings of the Lodge; to receive all moneys and pay them into the hands of the Treasurer."* The key to all this is, that he, the Secretary, is more than any other officer, save the Senior Deacon, under the immediate authority and direction of the Master. It is this that induces us to make a chapter of the Secretary's duties with a few hints relative to the Treasurer. It is but telling the Master what he should require the Secretary to do.

There is nothing that more clogs the wheels of a Lodge (or Grand Lodge) than to have the Secretary (or Grand Secretary)

---

* All that rubbish about "keeping the jewels bright" is the merest nonsense. It appears as if some Brethren adhere to a thing the more tenaciously the less sense or meaning there is in it. The responses of the Treasurer and Secretary are given literally in the *Monitor* in the Past Master's Degree, and those officers ought to be instructed by the Master to adhere to them,

set himself up as superior to the Master (or Grand Master.) It is in itself unnatural, and contrary to the spirit of the Masonic system of official gradation. It leads to nothing but evils, and the Master (or Grand Master) who suffers it deserves nothing but ignominy. Better change the Secretary (or Grand Secretary) every year than to allow it. Our American custom of changing our Masters (and Grand Masters) annually while Secretaries are retained in office, is leading to these unnatural results. But enough under this head. The Model Master, at least, will see that his Secretary does all his duty *and no more*, and the present chapter is designed to afford him some hints for that purpose.

And *first* it may be observed that the records are to be kept by the Secretary. As thare are many proceedings, however, that are not proper to be written, relating, as they do, to the esoteric or unpublished portions of Masonry, it is for the Master to decide what must be recorded and what omitted. This he does by turning from time to time to the Secretary and directing him to make record. For instance, suppose a Brother offers a motion to appropriate a sum of money. It is Seconded. The Master puts the motion in plain terms, then pauses and gives time for remarks *pro* and *con.* These being ended, he orders the vote. It is carried. And the Secretary makes the entry to correspond. To be sure that this entry is correct and that the Secretary has truly "observed the Worshipful Master's will and pleasure," the minutes of the Meeting are read aloud by the Secretary just prior to the closing of the

Lodge, and all errors and omissions, if any, are then corrected.*

A correct and complete *Form of Record* for a Lodge is a *desideratim* long acknowledged. In our publication, "The Secretary's Special Help," one will be found sufficiently elaborate for a model. An intelligent and experienced Secretary will enlarge upon it as he may deem necessary. The great aim of the Secretary should be to give a complete history of the doings of the Lodge, yet avoiding verbosity. At the opening of each Meeting, the names of all persons present, whether Officers, Past Masters or private members, must be noted. If visitors, the names, etc., of their respective Lodges must be noted; if demitted, the names of their late Lodges. † The doings of the Lodge are based upon 1 Motions or Resolutions, and 2 the Orders of the Master. The distinction between these two should be carefully drawn. For instance, suppose the Lodge has *adopted a Motion* "to receive a petition for Initiation." The Master upon that, *orders* a Committee to examine into the character of the applicant, and when the Com-

---

* It is not absolutely necessary that the Master should say in every case, "Brother Secretary record it." It is sufficient in all cases that the Secretary minute down every proceeding of the Lodge *as it falls from the lips of the Master;* yet it is better in the solution of all important questions, that the Master give direct orders to the Secretary as above.

† The *Model Master* will not have much visiting from Demitted Masons. They will learn from his remarks to his own brethren in how small repute he holds them as a class.

mittee has reported, *orders* the ballot spread. If the result is favorable he then *orders* the candidate to be brought forward for Initiation.

The Secretary is emphatically the *historian* of the Lodge; what the Lodge *does* is nothing unless *recorded.* The Secretary perpetuates the proceedings of the Craft. In the financials of the Lodge he bears an equally important part; what is *due* the Lodge is nothing unless *collected;* and the Secretary is that collector.

A proper system of collections involves punctuality; the dues of most of our Lodges are so insignificant in amount that the poorest can pay them if called for *monthly or quarterly.* The *Model Master*, therefore, will see that his Secretary makes a regular demand upon each member as often as every three months. If necessary, the By-Laws may be shaped to this end.

Under no circumstances will the Model Master allow his Lodge to get in debt. He will draw his orders upon the Treasurer at least quarterly for the stipend of the Secretary and Tyler, for Rents and all the current expenditures, and see that the Lodge does not fall behind.

The Secretary must be strongly charged with the necessity of paying over to the Treasurer all funds collected at least once a month. Failure to do this is a breach of contract with the Lodge, if not worse. The resources of the Lodge are only available when in the Treasurer's hands; to keep them in the Secretary's possession is but a snare to that officer and a fraud upon the Brethren who paid it into his hands. The evil is so frequent in practice as to demand special attention from the Master. The Minutes of each Meeting should specify how much money has been received since the last Meeting, and from whom.

The specific duties of the Secretary involve much labor in the intermissions, such as the collection of dues, taking evidence in trials, managing the correspondence, etc. It is, therefore, proper that he should have a pecuniary compensation for his services, and this compensation should be sufficiently large to secure good talent and experience.

Young Masters are often at a loss, when they have opened their Lodges, how to call up the proper business in due order. To remedy this, many Lodges adopt an "Order of business" for the Master's guide, though this is scarcely necessary. The reading of the Minutes of the last Regular* and intermediate Called Meetings will suggest the most important business of the Meetings, and the rest comes up in the form of Orders from the Master and Motions from the Brethren. The Model Master will require all Motions to be in writing and read aloud, not by their movers, but by the Secretary. †

---

* Some years since, we were deluded by a specious argument into using the term "stated" instead of "Regular." But we have since found in the oldest records that the term "Regular" is the ancient Masonic word, and we shall hereafter employ it.

† Referring, of course, to those that admit of being written. The Motion "to receive a Petition," etc., need not be in writing, because the Petition is in writing.

The most perfect confidence should exist between the Master and his Secretary. A good Secretary is the very light and salt of a Lodge, and the Master should set an example in showing how highly he is appreciated. Every reasonable demand of that officer should be granted. Ample stationery, cabinets, desks and the like should be provided him at his call.

But little need be said relative to the Treasurer. His duty is simple—to receive moneys from the Secretary and pay them out by order of the Master. It is important that he should be present at every meeting if possible. Where the funds of a Lodge accumulate to a considerable amount, the Model Master will advise the Treasurer to separate the Lodge funds from his own money, so that in the event of his (the Treasurer's) death, the Lodge may readily secure its own. The list of Lodges, bankrupted by the death of their Treasurers, is startling in magnitude, and suggests this as the proper remedy.

A word, also, relative to the Senior Deacon. He is strictly the appointee of the Master, * and is selected with a view to serve in all respects as *the Master's proxy.* An old and experienced active member makes the best Senior Deacon. He must be a polite, educated and zealous Brother. Between the Master and Senior Deacon there should exist unreserved confidence and mutual respect.

---

* If the By-Laws otherwise dispose of it, we suggest to the reader that upon the announcement of his election as Master, he should notify the brethren that he expects to have the privilege of *nominating* the Senior Deacon.

CHAPTER XII.

THE MASTER'S WAGES.

But why should a man take all this trouble upon himself, asks the reader who has followed us, patiently or impatiently, to this closing Chapter. What reward is there for this sacrifice of time, labor, patience, and feelings? Why depart from the "free and easy" system so much in vogue in the Lodges of the present day,—a fashion that costs the Master nothing but a little wear and tear of conscience, and twelve evenings in a year for Lodge purposes?

Really, we are not called upon by any sense of duty to answer such questions. For these XII Chapters are addressed to "Model Masters," men whose aims and desires are depictured in the First Chapter as being above those of the "herd of Masters" who seek the office, not that they may reflect credit upon the office, but that the office may reflect credit upon them. *But they miss both.*

Nevertheless, we will answer the question, because in so doing we can make a Chapter, our twelfth and last, upon "The Wages of the Model Master," in other words, "the rewards of well doing in the Masonic Temple." It is a pleasant theme; we will try and do it justice. Shall we commence it by giving three illustrations!

First.—The President of a popular Female College, a man crowded and overcrowded with the cares of his profession, devotes one evening per week, through two years of office, to building up, animating and instructing his Lodge. His reward is the love of his members, the name of a great and wise Mason resounding through all the land, and the acclamation of his Grand Lodge that advances him at once to high station and influence. Is not that ample wages?

Second.—A plain carpenter gives his hours to *study* over his saw and plane, and hours to instructing the Brethren who have honored him with the Master's gavel! For a year his efforts toward their improvement are unremitting and the incessant practice makes him what he desires others to be, "a Master in Israel." His reward is like that of the other, and there is no position of Masonic honor or usefulness that is not open to this plain but earnest mechanic. Is not the pay ample?

Third.—A physician in large practice. A man with a large family. A man busy with cares of church and state. Yet he finds time to study the true Rituals. He takes delight in them. They commend themselves to his judgment. He begins to teach them. He organizes a Home School of Instruction to teach them. From the heavy cares pressing upon him he steals an evening each week for the sweet task. His reward is a national reputation and, at the first suffrage, an election from the floor of the Grand Lodge to the position of Grand Master. Is not the reward ample?

We do not mean to imply that these examples exhaust the

subject; they scarcely dip into it. But they suggest in general terms what we consider *ample wages* to a faithful Master, viz.: the approbation of the Brethren, and a wide-spread appreciation of his labors. If that does not pay a disinterested and conscientious man for doing good to others, then he had best give his labor to some other Association than Masonry.

DeWitt Clinton, who was in many respects a "Model Master," the brightest in his generation, has stated the duties of, Masons and still more of Masters, clearly and succinctly. He says: "A Mason is bound to consult the happiness and promote the interests of his Brother; to avoid everything offensive to his feelings; to abstain from reproach, censure, and unjust suspicions; to warn him of the machinations of his enemies; to advise him of his errors; to advance the reputation and welfare of his family; to protect the chastity of his house; to defend his life, his property, and what is dearer to a man of honor, his *character* against unjust attacks; to relieve his wants and his distress; to instil into his mind proper ideas of conduct in the department of life which he is called to fill; and let me add, to foster his schemes of interest and promotion, if compatible with the paramount duties a man owes to the community." Now, all this goes to make up the prosperity of a Lodge, and if the Master, through his exertions as teacher and governor, sees these results of his care, the consciousness of it is a reward richer than the diamond mines of Golconda.

The wages of the Model Master are abundant, if his conscience approves his year's work. Upon setting out he made the following covenant with himself.

1. That I will perform all my official duties as between myself and my conscience, being guided therein by my Installation Covenant."—Have you done this? then the approbation of a good conscience is the very voice of God whispering in your heart.

" 2. That I will rule my Lodge without fear, favor, or hope of reward, save the approbation of my conscience and of God."—Have you done this? then the praises of your Brethren and the approbation of your Grand Lodge will be as sweet incense to you.

" 3. That I will endeavor to allure my Brethren to attend all the meetings of the Lodge by the allurements of abundant Masonic instruction for their wages."

" 4. That I will at all times and by all means seek for the ancient Work and Lectures of Masonry, and be satisfied with nothing less."

" 5. That the distressed, worthy Brother shall never go away disappointed from the door of my Lodge, if in my power to aid him."

" 6. That I will strive in knowledge, charity, truth, courtesy, and love to be a model to my Brethren."

" 7. That the evil doer under my jurisdiction shall have no rest until he reforms or is cut off."

" 8. That the officers under me shall each acquire and perform his duties accurately and thoroughly according to his Installation Covenant."

" 9. That my Lodge shall have honor and respect among its fellows."

In summing up, by these tables, your year's work as Master, your reward is in every memory of duty done. Every Brother, allured to come to the Lodge where he has learned to subdue his passions and improve himself in Masonry; every acquisi- tion made by yourself in the ancient and genuine Rituals; every distressed Brother relieved ; every evil doer reformed or cut off; every improvement made by the officers under you, whereby they have been made worthy to take in turn the gavel of Master, that so the good work may go on ; and every indication of honor and respect paid to your Lodge by other Lodges around you ; each of these is a unit in the aggregate sum of your reward. To know, too, that the year of your administration will be remembered as "the bright particular year" in the history of the Lodge; that your name will be marked with honor among the Past Masters; that in the Grand Lodge you will be deemed the representative of the best knowledge and zeal of your Lodge, and that when the acacia blooms above your your name and labors will be grate- fully cherished there—these are wages ample and rich to reward you for all that you have done.

So intimately connected with the "Master's Wages" is the "Wages of the Craft," that we add the following lines as a fitting close to the Chapter.

CORN, WINE, OIL.

They come from many a pleasant home,—
To do the Ancient Work they come
    With cheerful hearts and light ;
They leave the world without, a space,
And gathering here in secret place
    They spend the social night ;
They earn the meed of honest toil,
Wages of Corn and Wine and Oil.

Upon the sacred Altar lies,
Ah, many a precious sacrifice
    Made by these working men ;
The passions curbed, the lusts restrained,
And hands with human gore unstained,
    And hearts from envy clean ;
They earn the meed of honest toil,
Wages of Corn and Wine and Oil.

They do the deeds THEIR MASTER did ;
The naked clothe, the hungry feed—
    They warm the shivering poor :
They wipe from fevered eyes the tear ;
A Brother's joys and griefs they share,
    As ONE had done before ;
They earn the meed of honest toil,
Wages of Corn and Wine and Oil.

Then pay these men their just desert !
Let none dissatisfied, depart,
  But give them full reward ;
Give Light, that longing eyes may see ;
Give Truth, that will from error free ;
  Give them to know the LORD :—
Give them the meed of honest toil,
Wages of Corn and Wine and Oil.

Show them how Masons, Masons know,
The land of strangers journeying through ;
  Show them how Masons love ;
And let admiring spirits see
How reaches Masons' charity
  From earth to heaven above ;
Give them the meed of honest toil,
Wages of Corn and Wine and Oil.

Then will each Brother's tongue declare
How bounteous his Wages are,
  And Peace will reign within ;
Your walls with skillful hands will grow,
And coming generations know
  Your Temple is Divine ;
Then give the meed of honest toil,
Wages of Corn and Wine and Oil.

THE LODGE ROOM AND ITS FURNISHING.

The diagram and accompanying letter-press of a Lodge room will be found convenient to the Master in improving the appearance or increasing the work-facilities of his Lodge. When a Lodge-room is properly fitted up, the visitor entering at "13" sees the Junior Deacon immediately at his left hand. Beyond the Junior Deacon, and directly over his head the graceful ornamental tops of the elegant Pillars J. and B., are to be seen in range. Conspicuously displayed over the Master's chair is the Letter G. A handsome Altar, properly surmounted, rises before him. Over his left shoulder he sees the Senior Warden sitting on his two-graded dais, a small table or pedestal on his right. On the right of the visitor, and at the centre of the south wall of the apartment, sits the Junior Warden, a small table or pedestal on his right. On a commanding place over the Treasurer's head hangs the Emblematic Carpet. On a commanding place beyond the Secretary, rise the shelves of the Lodge-library. The *tout ensemble* is elegant and instructive

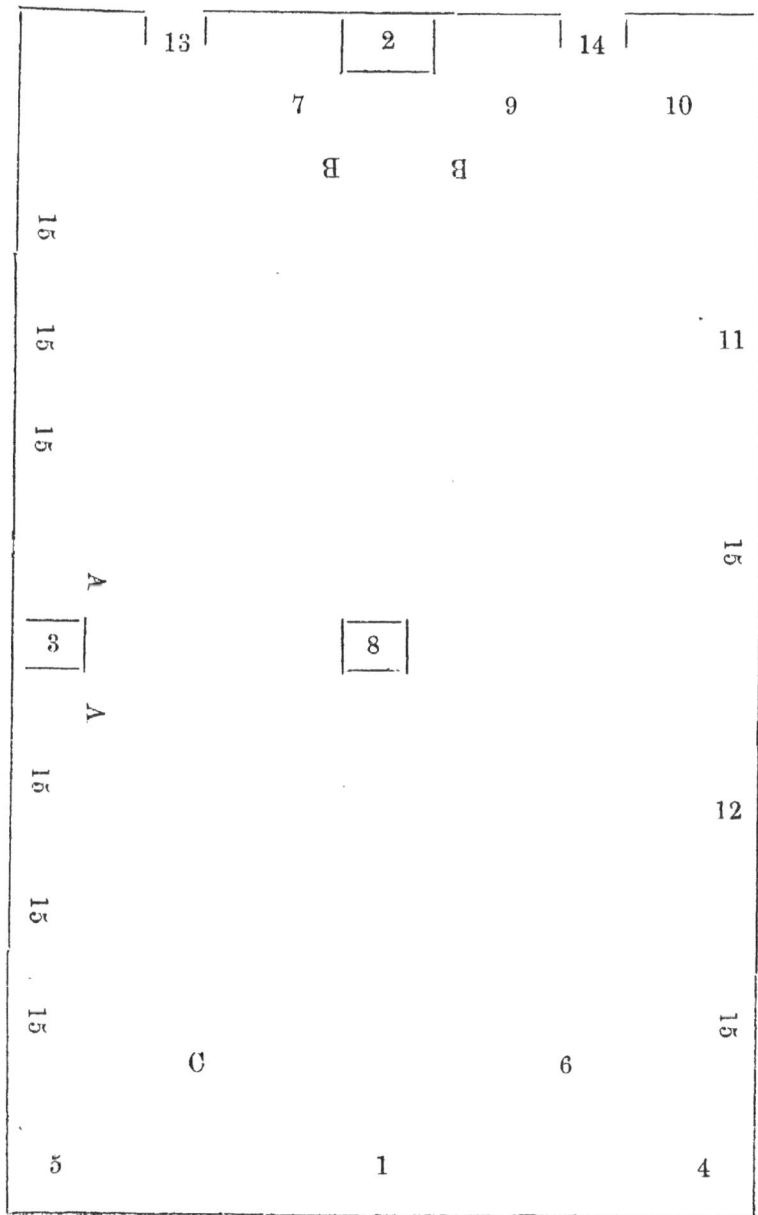

DIAGRAM.

| 13 | 2 | 14 |

7   9   10

B   B

15

15

15

15

A

3

A

8

15

11

15

12

15

15

C   6

5   1   4

DESCRIPTION OF THE FIGURE ON THE LAST PAGE.*

No. 1. *Station of the Master, usually termed the Dais.*—This is reached by an ascent of three steps. On his right and a little in front, is a small table holding the Gavel, etc. On his right and in line with his chair are seats for 4, 6, 8, or even more Past Masters, as the space may warrant.

No. 2. *Station of the Senior Warden.*—This is reached by an ascent of two steps. On his right and a little in front is a small table holding the Gavel, Column, etc. There is room on this platform for his own seat only.

No. 3. *Station of the Junior Warden.*—This is reached by an ascent of one step. On his right and a little in front is a small table holding the Gavel, Column, etc. There is room on his platform for his own seat only.

---

* When the fraternity are about to erect a Masonic Hall of their own, it is inexcusable not to arrange the entrances, etc., according to the proper system. Then the Tyler's door is on the Senior Warden's right, and the door of the Preparation Room on his left, all the other details corresponding. But where the fraternity are compelled, as is most frequently the case, to rent and fit up an apartment already built, they must do the best in regard to their entrances, they can, and the work of the Lodge must conform to that necessity. Thus it often hapens that the Master's station, *which is always the Masonic East of the Lodge*, does not correspond with the magnetic east, and the Tyler's door is near the S. E., N. W., or some other corner of the room.

No. 4. *Station of the Treasurer.**—Before him is a table supplied with stationery.

No. 5. *Station of the Secretary.**—Before him and at his left hand and rear, are all necessary desks with drawers and compartments for his books, papers, seal-press, and the Lodge Library.

No. 6. *The Chair of the Senior Deacon.*—Nearly in a line between the N. E. and S. W. corners of the room. Upon the chair are rings or catchers by which his rod can be held upright when not in use.

No. 7. *The Chair of the Junior Deacon.†*—This is arranged to hold his rod in the same manner as that of the Senior Deacon.

No. 8. *The Altar.*—The lesser lights are not shown in the figure, because there is no specific rule for placing them. Perhaps the best position for them is pendant immediately above the Altar.

---

* The portions of the eastern platform, or Dais, on which the Treasurer and Secretary sit, are not elevated so high as that on which the Master's chair is placed, nor quite so high as the platform of the Junior Warden. It is of medium height between the latter and the raised platform running round the room on which the private brothers sit.

† This is located in the figure upon the supposition that the entrances to the Lodge are correctly given. If not, then the Junior Deacon must change the position of his seat to correspond with that of the Tyler's door.

No. 9. *The Pillar J.**

No. 10. *The Pillar B.*

Nos. 11 and 12. *The Stoves.*—These should be removed from the apartment in warm weather.

No. 13. *The Tyler's Door of Entrance.*

No. 14. *Candidates' Door of Entrance.*

Nos. 15, 15, 15, 15, 15, *Seats of the Private Brethren.*†

Many Lodges are provided with accommodation for two *Stewards*, who sit on the right and left and a little in front of the Junior Warden. Their places are marked **A A.**

In the jurisdiction of the New York, and perhaps a few others, Lodges are provided with two *Masters of Ceremonies*, who sit on the right and left and a little in front of the Senior Warden. Their places are marked **B B.**

---

*These are correctly called "Pillars," not "Columns." See 1 Kings, VII. 21. The "Columns" are the small architectural objects used by the wardens to denote the condition of the craft, whether at labor or refreshment.

It is a serious error to place these Pillars anywhere save by the entrance to the Preparation Room.

† It is an excellent arrangement to have these seats upon platforms elevated about 6 or 8 inches above the floor; not quite so high as that on which the Secretary and Treasurer sit.

In the jurisdiction of Canada and all others practising the English Work,* the *last Past Master* is provided with a seat of honor, and takes a positive part in the ceremonies. He sits on the left and a little in front of the Master, his place being opposite that of the Senior Deacon who is on the right.† This is marked C.

The best place to hang Sherer's Carpet, if you have one, is on the wall on the right of the Treasurer.‡ There it should be protected from dust and light during the intervals between the meetings, by a thick screen of cloth or wall paper.

On the lower step of the Dais, on the Master's right and left, should be seen the two Ashlars, the Rough on the right, the Perfect on the left. These are almost indispensable in a

---

*It often happens that brethren from England, Canada, etc., fail to gain admission into our Lodges, because they seem unable to "pass an examination." This is not often their fault; nor does it argue their ignorance. Their work, especially *their mode of examination*, is essentially different from ours, and every American Lodge ought to be instructed under the authority of its Grand Lodge, *what is* the proper form of examination for brethren from those jurisdictions.

† The terms *right* and *left* are used in relation to the officer with whose names they are associated. In designating the right and left of King Solomon's Temple, the observer is supposed to be looking Eastward, having the South on his right.

‡ Bro. John Sherer, the veteran Masonic symbolist, whose labors in that department give him the title of a Masonic benefactor, has recently prepared the emblems and published them in better form than the gigantic and unwieldly charts so long in vogue. This is not the place to describe the great improvements he has made.

Lodge. Upon the former, the three emblems, representing Freedom, Fervency and Zeal are placed.

The ballot-box, that Ægis of Masonic protection, is best kept under the Treasurer's desk. The Working Tools should lie on the lower step of the Dais, near the rough Ashlar.

Having thus sketched the more common arrangements of the room, we give a word of directions regarding the Tyler's room. This should be supplied with racks for hats and coats, a stove for cold weather, water, and a good number of seats for visiting brethren and members of the Lodge while awaiting permission to enter. A copy of the Holy Scriptures is a ne- cessary part of the Tyler's furniture. A Record Book for visiting brothers ; a copy of the Lodge By-laws, and catalogues of Lodges in your own State and other States, will be found convenient. Finally, a few toilet articles will not be amiss to those who wish to show as much respect for a Masonic Lodge as they would to a church.*

---

* In many of the Canada Lodges the brethren make it a point to attend dressed in white cravats, dress coats, etc., as scrupulously as though they were going to a ball. Is not this creditable to them ?

LIST OF GRAND MASTERS.

The following catalogue of Grand Masters is corrected up to March 1866. So many Masters of Lodges are in the pleasent habit of corresponding with these dignitaries on questions of a Masonic character that we deem it to be an acceptable addition to the " Special Help."

Alabama, WILSON WILLIAMS.

California, G. B. CLAIBORNE.

Canada, Wm. B. SIMPSON, Kingston.

Colorado, ANDREW MASON.

Connecticut, ELI S. QUINTARD.

Delaware, JOHN A. NICHOLSON, Dover,

District of Columbia, GEO. C. WHITING.

England, The EARL OF ZETLAND.

Florida, SAMUEL BENEZET, Tallahassee.

Georgia, JOHN HARRIS.

Illinois, H. P. H. BROMWELL.

Indiana, H. G. HAZELRIGG, Lebanon.

Iowa, EDWARD A. GUILBERT, Dubuque.

Ireland, The DUKE OF LEINSTER.

Kansas, JACOB SAQUI, Leavenworth.

Kentucky, M. J. WILLIAMS.

Louisiana, J. Q. A. FELLOWS, New Orleans.

Maine, Wm. P. PREBLE, Portland.

Maryland, JOHN COATES, Baltimore.

Massachusetts, CHARLES C. DAME, Boston:

Michigan, S. C. COFFINBURY, Constantine.

Mississippi, W. S. PATTON.

Missouri, JOHN F. HOUSTON, Richmond.

Nebraska, R. W. FURNAS.

Nevada, JOSEPH DE BELL.

New Hampshire, J. EVERETT SARGENT.

New Jersey, WM. J. WHITEHEAD, Newark.

New York, ROBERT D. HOLMES, New York.

North Carolina, JOHN McCORMICK.

Ohio, THOMAS SPARRRW, Columbus.

Oregon, S. F. CHADWICK.

Pennsylvania, LUCIUS H. SCOTT, Philadelphia.

Rhode Island, THOMAS A. DOYLE, Providence.

Scotland, J. WHYTE MELVILLE.

South Carolina, JAMES L. ORR.

Tennessee, THOMAS A. HAMILTON, Memphis.

Texas, R. M. ELGIN.

Vermont, L. B. ENGLESBY, Burlington.

Washington Territory, ASA L. BROWN.

West Virginia, W. J. BATES.

Wisconsin, JOHN T. WENTWORTH. *

* As the Post Office address of many of these names is omitted, it will usually suffice to direct a letter to the Grand Master by name, adding "Care of the Grand Secretary, Grand Lodge of Freemasons, of the State of ——," and sending it, thus directed, to the seat of Government of the State.

FAREWELL.

And now Worshipful Brother, farewell. Having gone with you, bit by bit, through all the details of your official duty, having advised, warned, and rebuked with the freedom of the editorial pen, let us, in the loving spirit of the Past Master, wish that you may be one of the "Ghiblim," indeed, a "Stone Squarer," in whom there is no defect; and whose wages shall be the love and gratitude of his fellows, and the evident approval of the Grand Overseer!

So MOTE IT BE with us when life shall end,
And from the East, the LORD OF LIGHT shall bend,
And we, our six days' labor fully done,
Shall claim our wages at the MASTER's throne.

So MOTE IT BE with us: that when the Square,
That perfect implement, with heavenly care,
Shall be applied to every block we bring,
No fault shall see our MASTER and our KING.

So MOTE IT BE WITH US: that though our days
Have yielded little to the MASTER's praise,
The little we *have* builded may be proved
To have the marks our first GRAND MASTER loved.

So MOTE IT BE WITH US: we are but weak ;
Our days are few ; our trials who can speak !
But sweet is our communion while we live,
And rich rewards the MASTER deigns to give.

Let's toil then, cheerfully, let's die in hope ;
The WALL in wondrous grandeur riseth up ;
They who come after shall the work complete,
And they and we receive the WAGES meet.

THE FIVE POINTS OF FELLOWSHIP.

The following, from a publication of 1826, is a golden fragment :

" When the necessities of a Brother call for my aid and support, I will be ready to render him such assistance to save him from sinking, as may not be detrimental to myself or connexions, if I find him worthy thereof.

Indolence shall not cause my footsteps to halt nor wrath turn them aside ; but forgetting every self consideration, I will be ever swift of foot to serve, help, an execute benevolence to a fellow-creature in distress ; and more particularly to a Brother Mason.

When I offer up my ejaculations to Almighty God, a Brother's welfare will I remember as my own ; for as the voice of babes and sucklings ascends to the throne of grace, so most assuredly do the breathings of a fervent heart arise to the mansions of bliss, as our prayers are certainly required of each other.

A Brother's secrets delivered to me as such, I will keep as I would my own ; as betraying my trust might be doing him the greatest injury he could sustain in this mortal life ; nay, it would be like the villainy of an assassin, who lurks in darkness to stab his adversary.

A Brother's character I will support in his absence as I would in his presence ; I will not wrongfully revile him myself, nor will I suffer it to be done by others, if in my power to prevent it.

Thus, by the Five Points of Fellowship, are we linked together in one indivisible chain of sincere affection, brotherly love, relief, and truth."

INDEX.

——o——

www.ingramcontent.com/pod-product-compliance
Lightning Source LLC
Chambersburg PA
CBHW031436270326
41930CB00007B/726